ArtScroll Series®

Rabbi Nosson Scherman / Rabbi Meir Zlotowitz

General Editors

Roiza D. Weinreich

W.H.A.T.

WORDS HABITS ACTIONS THOUGHTS

CAN RELIEVE

Published by

Mesorah Publications, ltd

STRESS

Practical and effective ways to ease stress and celebrate life

FIRST EDITION
First Impression … September 1998

Published and Distributed by
MESORAH PUBLICATIONS, LTD.
4401 Second Avenue / Brooklyn, N.Y 11232

Distributed in Europe by
J. LEHMANN HEBREW BOOKSELLERS
20 Cambridge Terrace
Gateshead, Tyne and Wear
England NE8 1RP

Distributed in Israel by
SIFRIATI / A. GITLER
10 Hashomer Street
Bnei Brak 51361

Distributed in Australia and New Zealand by
GOLDS BOOK & GIFT SHOP
36 William Street
Balaclava 3183, Vic., Australia

Distributed in South Africa by
KOLLEL BOOKSHOP
Shop 8A Norwood Hypermarket
Norwood 2196, Johannesburg, South Africa

Typography by CompuScribe at ArtScroll Studios, Ltd.

Printed in the United States of America by Noble Book Press Corp.
Bound by Sefercraft, Quality Bookbinders, Ltd., Brooklyn N.Y. 11232

This book is dedicated

to my grandfather

הרב משה בן הרב ברוך הכהן זצ״ל

Moshe Kessler

and my grandmother

מחלה בת הרב צבי יהודה ז״ל

Machla Kessler

Zeidy was born to a home of Torah. At the age of 12 he had achieved such deep Torah learning that three *rebbis* came and said they had no more Torah to teach him. He got his *semichah* at the age of 16. His grandfather and many of his uncles were *rabbonim*. During World War I, he was forced to wander away from home and family to escape being drafted into the Russian and Austrian Army. When he approached Lublin, he hired himself out to chop wood. He learned *Gemara* by heart with his cousin Avraham Ackerman. When the *Rosh Yeshivah* overheard their Torah learning, he called to them to stop chopping wood and join his students.

Right after he got married, Zeidy went to buy furniture, but he saw a beautiful set of *Shas* and brought home three crates of Torah volumes instead of the dining-room table and chairs.

Zeidy was a *gabbai* in the Trisker *shul* in Dubno. Every day he woke up at 5 o'clock in the morning to learn Torah. Each winter he supplied wood for the *shul*. He was a leader of the

Dubno community to whom many turned for guidance, strength and support until the very last difficult moments of the *churban* in Europe. Hundreds of people came to him each week for help, and his motto was never to turn away a Jew empty-handed. His wise foresight saved the lives of his children.

On the day he died he told a fellow Jew who was hiding together with him in a bunker, "You are young and alone. Get out now and run. Run away and try to survive. Hashem will be with you. I cannot leave," Zeidy said, "because everyone is depending on me." This man lived.

My grandfather and grandmother Kessler were killed on Simchas Torah in 1942.

May Hashem avenge their blood.

Our ancestors fought to hold onto Torah and *mitzvos* through many difficult tribulations. Their legacy of Torah and *chesed* continues to live on in their children, grandchildren and great-grandchildren. May our Torah learning and *mitzvos* be a merit for them and for all the *kedoshim*.

ACKNOWLEDGMENTS

I would like to thank the many people who provided ideas and support during the process of writing this book.

My sister Manya Fisher helped tremendously in bringing this book to you. My appreciation goes to all the participants in my workshops who generously shared their life's experience. As our sages said in Avos, "From my students I learned the most." This book includes the stories and poetry of three friends and writing colleagues. Thank you to Gitty Kar, Malkie Treitel and Cipory Weber.

Mrs. Ethel Gottlieb was thorough yet gentle while editing. Her insight and creative ideas added profoundly to the book. It was truly delightful and encouraging to work with her.

Gratitude goes to Rabbis Meir Zlotowitz and Nosson Scherman for putting their faith in this project and for their help in bringing about the impressive success of my first three books. My special thanks to Rabbi Sheah Brander whose expert knowledge and creativity made the book complete. Thank you to Rabbi Eli Kroen. Rabbi Avrohom Biderman is efficient yet sensitive; my thanks for his insight and helpfulness. My appreciation to Mrs. Mindy Stern, Mrs. Judy Dick, Miss Hindy Goldner, Mrs. Mindy Schwartz, Mrs. Toby Goldzweig, Mrs. Toby Akerman, Miss Rifky Bruck, Miss Chumie Zaidman, and Shaya Sonnenschein of the ArtScroll staff. I consider it a privilege to participate in the ArtScroll Series.

My parents, Mr. and Mrs. Moshe Perlman, and my mother-in-law, Mrs. Pearl Weinreich, have encouraged and sustained all my various undertakings. I hope they will always have *nachas* from all their children and grandchildren. The first one to read significant portions of the book was my husband Faivel. From that beginning he's helped me decide many times what will work and what won't and has patiently encouraged me not to give up when I faced minor setbacks.

On Monday morning I wake up at 7 a.m. I open my eyes and I walk over to my son's bed and tell him that it's time to wake up to say *Shema* with his father in *shul*, with a *minyan*. Afterwards he will go to learn *Gemara* in yeshivah. "Sholom, wake up to learn. Your learning is special. It's because you wake up now to learn every day that we are able to have a big *Siyum HaShas*." Sholom sits up and looks at me skeptically. "Sholom, don't you see. Zeidy and Bubby came here from Poland alone after the *churban* in Europe. It is only because they and hundreds of other parents woke up boys like you to go to yeshivah that we have a *siyum* in which 50,000 Jews participated. The fathers who learn *Daf Yomi* today were once young boys. From single individuals the flame of Torah was rekindled. Now the spark continues on with you, you are helping it grow bigger."

This book is dedicated to my parents and your parents who survived the *churban* in Europe. Can we measure the treasures that the generation that survived the *churban* in Europe has given us? How many of Hashem's commandments can we accomplish easily because our parents paved the way? How many priceless lessons did our parents teach us? May they continue to encourage us in good health.

My parents, along with the entire generation that survived the *churban,* teach by example. There aren't enough words to describe their lessons adequately. They teach courage, joy in life, selfless giving, and gratitude for life's blessings. These are their priorities. They never seek honor. Torah and *mitzvos* are the most important joy. Life is precious and children are most precious of all. The greatest privilege is the ability to give selflessly and anonymously to a Jew in need.

How many mothers are we? Every day hundreds of thousands of mothers wake up to say *Shema* and to encourage their husbands and children to learn Torah. Hashem, help us to remember on the sunny days and on the rainy days why we are working so hard to perpetuate the learning of Your Torah. Master of the Universe, May it be Your will that the Torah sparks our parents kindled burn brightly for all the generations, until the speedy redemption.

I thank Hashem for the wide acceptance of my first three books and for the *zechus* to reach thousands of people around the world with Torah ideas that helped them to be better Jews.

וִיהִי נֹעַם ה׳ אֱלֹקֵינוּ עָלֵינוּ
וּמַעֲשֵׂה יָדֵינוּ כּוֹנְנָה עָלֵינוּ וּמַעֲשֵׂה יָדֵינוּ כּוֹנְנֵהוּ

May Hashem's presence and satisfaction rest upon us. May Hashem complete our efforts and assure their success. May the work of our hands establish Hashem's Kingdom on earth.

TABLE OF CONTENTS

INTRODUCTION   vii

PART ONE

WORDS

ONE	INNER NOISE	13
TWO	LEARN HOW TO TALK TO YOUR EMOTIONS	23
THREE	RESISTING INSULT WHEN OTHERS ARE NOT SUPPORTIVE	37
FOUR	SUNSHINE, RAIN AND WORDS	53
FIVE	TWELVE QUICK TIPS TO HELP YOU MANAGE STRESS	59

HABITS

SIX	DECISIONS: MAKING BETTER CHOICES	65
SEVEN	FLEXIBILITY — THE ANTIDOTE TO PERFECTIONISM	71
EIGHT	FAITH — THE OXYGEN OF THE SOUL	83
NINE	GRATITUDE — MY LITTLE BOOK OF MAGIC	91
TEN	SMART HABITS FOR STRESSFUL TIMES	101

ACTIONS

ELEVEN	SERENITY THROUGH SIMPLICITY	107
TWELVE	DO WHAT YOU CAN	119
THIRTEEN	TERRIFIC PEOPLE	125
FOURTEEN	ONE TYPE OF WORRY THAT HELPS	137
FIFTEEN	COPING WITH THE AFTERNOON SLUMP	143
SIXTEEN	ACTION CHECKLIST	149

THOUGHTS

SEVENTEEN	STRENGTH THROUGH PRAYER	153

EIGHTEEN   SHORTCUTS TO HAPPINESS   165
NINETEEN   REMINDING YOURSELF   173

PART TWO

UPLIFTING TREATS FOR YOU   177
THE LAST WORD   223

A CALM HEART
W.H.A.T. CAN RELIEVE STRESS

This is a book about stress. When you are in a stressful situation do you say, "I don't know what to do"? Often this means that you want to do something to modify everybody else's actions to your liking. Your mother, father, spouse, child, neighbor, friend, boss or teacher must change so that *your* life can be free of stress. Reforming others around you in order to relieve worry and anxiety only *appears* to work. For a while superficial suggestions will work, but never for more than a week or two. If you want to have a harmonious life, instead of one filled with anxiety and tension, then **you** are the one who must act.

If you have previously tried to change your actions you may be feeling discouraged. Real change takes effort, and there seem to be many impenetrable barriers facing you before you even begin. The Chofetz Chaim quotes the *Zohar HaKadosh* to assure us that when we strive to improve our character we are not working alone. Hashem helps us unlock the chains that have bound us and assists us so we can become a different person.

> We have learned that one's actions below on earth awaken Hashem's response Above. When one does a good deed, a corresponding positive force is activated Above. If a man performs an act of kindness in the world, he, in turn, arouses kindness in Hashem toward the world on that day. The day is crowned with compassion in this man's merit. That day becomes a shield for the person when he is in need of protection.

In the way that a person acts, they act towards him in Heaven. Fortunate is the one who acts properly, because it is clear that one's deeds create a corresponding chord Above (*Sefer Shemiras HaLashon*, Chofetz Chaim).

Are you prepared to learn W.H.A.T. you can do about stress?

This book can help you create a more serene life. Simply cultivate any of the four areas of your life that are represented in the following pages. The word **W.H.A.T.** alludes to these four areas. **W.** stands for the **words** we speak to ourselves and to others. **H.** stands for positive **habits** that can enhance our daily routine. **A.** stands for **action** — instead of worrying, do something concrete even if it's a small thing. **T.** stands for **thought**. Focusing on beneficial thoughts will broaden our horizons. Letting go of negative beliefs will give us renewed vitality.

My writing is a good example of the power of W.H.A.T. — Words, Habits, Actions and Thought. Most readers assume that I was born with a talent for writing. Actually writing is my hidden talent. Writing is one area of my life where I had to overcome obstacles by using **Words** to find self-confidence and develop the **Habit** of writing, although I couldn't do it perfectly. I demonstrated **Action** when I wrote something *every* day, even if it was one page. Finally I used the power of **Thought**. I was only able to develop ideas and write them down because I was willing to struggle when I began. There is a transitional period between one's old and new belief systems. The following are some thoughts about writing that I had to overcome.

During my school years every composition and book report was an arduous mountain to climb. From the day the report was assigned I worried about my teacher's stringent standards. At the same time, however, I designated many hours to develop possible ideas and to write and rewrite. Yet, for all my effort, my teacher never gave me that coveted A+.

My elementary-school teacher knew all about writing. She explained that every part of a sentence has its place. We would diagram a sentence — i.e., make the sentence into a small map. The prepositional phrase had its path. The nouns were placed in a box — like a little house. The verbs were circled, resembling a plot of grass.

My teacher knew all about writing. She knew about commas, periods, semi-colons, and proper spelling. It was very important never to confuse an adverb with an adjective. My teacher was an expert at tenses. There was the present and the present perfect, the past and the future. Every sentence in the paragraph must match.

I tried so hard. I envisioned ideas and created original characters. I wrote a few lines, crumpled up my paper and began again. I worked for hours, but she never gave me more than a B+.

When I initially met the editor who would work with me on my first book, I felt anxious about my present perfect, my adjectives, my quotation marks and my commas. Fayge said with a laugh, "Those are the easiest things to fix. Writing isn't about perfect grammar — it's about good ideas."

I am very grateful for the gift of writing. About once a week a letter arrives in the mail from someone who read a book of mine. I realize that *Baruch Hashem* I am helping people to see things in new ways. Through my books I can reach and teach thousands of people how to apply Torah thoughts to their daily lives and thereby find satisfaction in life. Often the letters ask, "When are you writing another book?"

Writing about Torah topics has pushed me to learn new things every day. Learning Torah doesn't stop with 12th grade. I hope that through my book you will see that Torah thoughts can be applied to your daily life. I hope you will be encouraged to learn a little bit every day.

You will achieve the quickest results if you are consistent with the exercises in the book. I hope my book will fascinate and entertain. Please read it in your favorite room. Comfortable surroundings are conducive to concentration and will make the mental exercise more pleasant.

When you read a chapter make it a priority. You don't have to hire a babysitter, and you don't have to travel for three hours — but you do have to arrange not to be interrupted by the phone or visitors. Cook supper before you sit down to read and don't take out your knitting until you finish.

Have you ever seen a sign near an escalator that read, "Be kind to your heart. Use the steps"? When the magic escalator steps carry you, you reach your destination quickly, but if you want to grow, you have to use the "muscles" of your own mind. Do the exercises. They are easy and won't take a lot of time. If you glance at them and say, "I'll do this later," you are missing out on the main advantage of the book.

If you have enough willpower, do the exercises before you read the "True Responses" so that your thinking will not be influenced by other people's suggestions.

Your retention will be better if you pause and regroup at the end of each chapter. Review the material in your mind. Take a walk around the room or around the block.

Success has less to do with the actual ability you have right now than with your desire and determination. You don't even have to do a lot at one time, but your effort must be sincere. As Dorothy Tennov, says in *Super-Self,* a step toward your goal "should be large enough to be discernible, small enough to be accomplished."

Enjoy!

GOALS

Here is a list of the areas we will be working on in this book. Use numbers to indicate which areas you would most like to work on, in order of priority.

I would like to ...

_____ FOCUS ON THE POSITIVE IN MYSELF

_____ FIND COURAGE TO TRY NEW TECHNIQUES

_____ STOP WAKING UP IN THE MIDDLE OF THE NIGHT

_____ DO AWAY WITH THE WORRY HABIT

_____ ENJOY MY LIFE MORE

_____ HANDLE PROBLEMS WELL

_____ LEARN TO MAKE DECISIONS

_____FIND INNER SERENITY

_____ OTHER

WORDS

HABITS

ACTIONS

THOUGHTS

Chapter One

Inner Noise

Inner Noise
by Malky Farkas Treitel

I have to insert
a different tape.
My mind
is playing
the wrong one.

It's the one
that makes me
feel awkward,
like a stranger
living in
my own skin.

All these years,
that tape still
stealthily
inserts itself
and catches me
by surprise.

I think this poem applies to us all. Don't we all deal with inner noise? Some of us are so bothered by inner noise that we prefer keeping busy all day to avoid listening to it. When we struggle to calm our heart, our thoughts continue to whisper incessantly inside us.

I am usually the first to wake up in my house. If I'm up early enough I can actually see a patch of the sunrise from my window. At such times I remain in bed for a few moments and just listen to the quiet around me. I can't believe that there is total silence in all the rooms. I hear only gentle whispering sounds — of children breathing quietly, beds creaking, the rustle of leaves, birds chirping outside and the slow dripping of a faucet.

There are many voices in my mind. My inner voice tells me that already I have woken up too late and that I am behind schedule before my day has even begun. An imaginary child's voice pipes up, "Didn't you promise we would go for a walk outdoors today?" A screen turns on with images of today's chores — everything from laundry to writing to picking up clothes from the cleaners. The worry bus stops to honk and unload a carload of creatures that buzz around. I worry about insults I've heard and difficult people I've met and my children's difficult teachers and my sister's flu. What can I do about all these worries?

I had thought it was quiet, yet suddenly I feel overwhelmed by noise. Where can a moment of peaceful serenity be found? Can I possibly find a quiet moment within? Should I simply wait for these feelings to disappear? Do I want to carry these sentiments, resounding inside me, all day? The books say, "Imagine the ocean." Can *you* visualize the ocean at seven in the morning?

Our world is a cacophony of sound. When we are busy we don't hear it, but whenever we try to calm down, we realize how much noise there is. Not only that — every sound seems magnified. The blaring car alarms, clanking snow plows, and clanging and screeching trains seem to be right there in the room with us. Even in our houses, the normal everyday noises wake us up or keep us from falling asleep — the creak of the stairs, the banging of the radiator, the baby's whimper or the clicking of the computer printer if our spouse is working late. Do we remember in the middle of the day that the dripping faucet or the creaking door hinge should be taken care of or do we notice it only at 2 a.m.?

Just as physical noise affects us, the internal noises that our minds create influence us as well. In his chapter on "Watchfulness," Rabbi Moshe Chaim Luzzatto, author of *Mesillas Yesharim* says, "This is one of the clever devices of the evil inclination — to mount constant pressure on the hearts and minds of men until they don't have a calm moment to consider and observe the type of life they are leading." Our hearts and minds are always working. There is an incessant stream of thoughts, yearnings, and cravings. The evil inclination keeps us busy with thinking instead of doing. Our thoughts carry us to places we may not wish to go. At the same time there is a productive area that is closed off. Do we really need these worries? Is it beneficial to be upset and concerned? Elaine, one of our workshop participants, had an insightful comment that initiated a lively discussion: "I'm always aggravating myself. I feel like a broken record. I just can't relax."

During the day our hands keep on moving and our feet rush from one errand to another. We may forget where we have put things because of the background noise in our heads, but we do continue to function automatically. However, when we attempt to remain quiet for a few moments all the distressing thoughts and feelings begin to buzz like a swarm of flies that refuse to go away.

I asked the group, "Have you ever felt like a broken record?"

HAVE YOU EVER FELT LIKE A BROKEN RECORD?

_____

_____

_____

_____

_____

_____

_____

Remember, each person reacts differently to life's "inner noises" that often prevent us from living life to its fullest. I have found it encouraging to hear the different reactions when we read the participant's responses aloud in the group. When you discover that you can easily shut off some thoughts that are causing you discomfort, you realize that you are not helpless. You may also find ideas you can use when reading about others in similar circumstances.

How do you feel about each of these situations? Respond with the first thought that comes to mind — be it a reaction or a solution.

1. **Parent's call:** At 11 p.m. your mother or father calls and talks to you for ten minutes about everything you do wrong.

When you hang up the phone, you _____

_____

2. **Teenager's announcement:** Your teenager walks in after school and says, "By the way, Ma, the principal wants to see you tomorrow."

When you hear this news, you _____

_____

3. **Husband out working late:** Your husband calls and says, "I'll be working until about 2 a.m., but there's no reason for you to stay up waiting for me"

When you climb into bed, you _____

_____

4. **Cleaning help cancels:** At 7 p.m. the cleaning help calls to cancel. The next day you are hosting a party for thirty couples in your home, and you have no idea how you will manage on your own.

When you hang up, you _____

_____

5. **Child's stitches:** Your child fell late in the evening and you decided the wound didn't need stitches, although the cut is fairly deep.

When you climb into bed, you _____

_____

6. **Friend's engagement:** Your best friend calls at work to tell you that she got engaged and the engagement party is on Sunday.

As you stare at your computer screen, you _____

_____

7. **Prank caller:** The phone rings at 2 a.m. You pick it up and repeatedly ask who it is. The only response is heavy breathing.

When you hang up, you _____

_____

8. **Job interview:** You have a job interview for a position you are really interested in at 9 a.m. tomorrow.

As you do the housework, you _____

_____

9. **Labor alarm:** You are in the fourth week of your ninth month and when you lie down to sleep you feel a funny cramping sensation.

As you lie in bed, you _____

_____

10. **Lost pen:** You go shopping on Thursday night and after signing your check you leave a twenty-dollar pen at the checkout counter.

When you get home, you _____

_____

11. **Visit to the doctor:** You have a doctor's appointment this afternoon for a routine checkup.

When you wake up your first thoughts are _____

_____

Actual Responses

Keep your thumb in the previous page so that you can refer to the situations. Do you identify with any of the following true responses? Each quote is from a different person.

1. Parent's call —

- "I'm too tired. I'll worry about it at another time."
- "I don't know how I'd feel. I probably wouldn't be able to stop thinking about it, it would bother me."
- "My mother passed away this year. Many times I wake up at 2 a.m. thinking about things my mother wanted to do in her lifetime that we never did together. You might think it's an illogical thing to say, but I even miss the arguments we had."

2. Teenager's announcement —

- "Our children's lives are very tied up with our egos. It's hard to separate their successes, failures, and problems from our own."
- "I could think that it's their problem and not mine, but it probably wouldn't help."

3. Husband out working late —

- "My problem is slightly different. I try to wait up for my husband but most nights he gets home and finds that I've fallen asleep on the couch."
- "I can't fall asleep when my husband is not home. It's not that I'm afraid of anything happening, I just don't feel comfortable."
- "When my husband is out working late I may doze off, but my ears are tuned in. After a while, I hear the car locks beep and the scrape of the garbage can on the sidewalk outside and my muscles fall slack. Then I hear the gate clang and the lock snap. Finally, I hear the doorknob click and the keys jingle as they are put back in his pants pocket. Those sounds are like a lullaby. By the time he gets to the top step, I feel calm and relaxed."

4. Cleaning help cancels —

- "I go over in my mind or make a written list of how I will manage to do it all myself. Then I feel better."
- "I'm used to her canceling; it happens all the time! I put on my roller skates and get to work. I'd rather get something done right now than leave it all for tomorrow."
- "What cleaning lady? I don't have a cleaning lady, so I can't relate to this."
- "When the cleaning help doesn't come everyone in the family has to pitch in. They'll usually complain, 'Why can't the cleaning lady do this?' I say, 'What's wrong with you?' When they've finished and it wasn't as hard as they thought, they say, 'You pay someone to do this every week?' "

5. Child's stitches—

- "This would keep me up. I never trust my instincts when I think my child is not sick enough to take to the doctor."
- "I'll probably feel guilty — maybe it does, maybe it doesn't. It would keep me up for awhile."
- "I would have brought him to several friends who are experts in stitches to decide."

6. Friend's engagement—

- "I'd be so excited, I probably couldn't continue my work. This actually happened a long time ago, thank G–d, and my friend has three kids now."
- "I'd continue working while thinking happy, cozy thoughts."

7. Prank caller —

- "I'd unplug the phone for a few hours."
- "I probably would be afraid for a while, but if it does not happen again, I would forget about it."
- "I'd take the phone off the hook and remind myself that there are weird people out there."
- "I'd take the phone off the hook before I fell asleep each night for the rest of the month."

8. Job interview—
- "I would probably be nervous."
- "I'm very nervous, about the trial position they have given me. If they are happy with my work I will get a steady job. It's teaching an 'English as a Second Language' course. The students are between fifty and eighty. They intimidate me. So I say, 'Please G–d, I must have some sleep,' and after that I fall asleep."

9. Labor alarm—
- "I would be able to fall asleep because I know when it's the real thing I would definitely wake up. I always did!"
- "I would sleep now because who knows when I'll get another full night's sleep."
- "We got up and ran."

10. Lost Pen —
- "It's hard for me not to get into a lot of guilt. I'd ask myself, 'Why were you careless?' "
- "If it's very important to me I'd replace it right away. Once I replace it I don't worry about it."
- "I always say, 'Let it be a *kapparah* (atonement).' "

11. Visit to the Doctor—
- "Going to the doctor has always made me feel edgy because I feel totally helpless there. Everything about the doctor's office says, 'I'm the doctor, and you don't know anything.' The doctor I'm using now has me weigh myself and do some tests on my own. That makes me feel much more comfortable. They actually trust me to look at a strip and read results and to know my own weight. Now I can relax before my appointments. In this place, they treat you like a grownup."
- "I'd probably have problems feeling calm."
- "If it's a routine checkup, I wouldn't worry."
- "When I am worried about something serious, I start thinking about cooking, baking and things that I enjoy — this takes my mind off my concerns."

Although in a few instances people were able to tell themselves, "Worrying now won't help so I'll stop," the majority of responses attested to the fact that we don't feel comfortable when we are weighed down by worries.

Has this ever happened to you? You wake up feeling chilly and you put on a heavy turtleneck sweater. During the day you may find yourself in a doctor's office or an apartment where the heat is on a high setting. The heavy sweater itches and makes you feel uncomfortable. You feel stifled. Although you try to focus on what's happening right now in the room you can't escape the discomfort.

When unwanted thoughts overtake us it's difficult to cast them off. Comments like "I could think that everything will be all right, but it wouldn't help me," or, "I never trust my instincts," or "I'd be feeling nervous" reflect a common truth that our feelings *do* affect us.

This session usually brings a sense of relief to workshop participants. When we find out that everyone is plagued by worries now and then, we realize that our stress is not a foreign monster but a symptom of human existence. We recognize that we have a lot in common with others and that makes us feel less vulnerable and alone.

All of us must remember to trust our ability to help ourselves. After all, you have done your best with the knowledge you had up to this point. I was fascinated to learn techniques that allow me to communicate with the non-dominant part of my brain. It has helped me understand myself better. There is no better place to seek out helpful ideas than in the calm personal place inside yourself that you will discover. As you begin the journey and learn how to communicate with your emotions your life will improve.

Chapter Two
Learn How to Talk to Your Emotions

For the Sabbath, Reb Aryeh would put on a long coat that was old and worn, but clean and spotless. His shirt too was far from new, but always freshly starched and ironed silken-smooth. Once he explained to his son Chaim Yaakov why he preferred these clothes: "You see, my son, when you put on a new garment, you have to be careful not to get it dirty. When you wear old clothing, however, you learn to clean stains."

Was it not symbolic? All his life he worked at cleaning stains, not only his own but others' as well. Gently, delicately he cleansed human spirits ... (*A Tzaddik in Our Time,* p. 409).

I want to have a spotless personality. I want to be sure I am doing everything properly right now. However, it isn't something that happens automatically, rather it is a complex process of facing challenges and "cleansing stains." Do you feel that you can be "friends" with your many diverse aspects? Can you experience your feelings or do you bury them? Have you ever experienced being two different people?

Throughout the week, we want to retain that exalted feeling of inner calm that we experience when we light the Shabbos candles. What stops us is our inability to communicate our lofty thoughts directly to our emotions. Sometimes our emotions are so intense that we can't contain them. Our face may look different, our eyes may be sad, and we may need some quiet. On the surface it seems that all we have to do is ignore our emotions, carry on and cope, but in actuality this doesn't work. Our emotions are still there.

My husband described this phenomenon with an anecdote that has become a classic in his family. A cousin arrived at his home from out of town. The cousin was going to meet a New York girl that night and he used their house as his headquarters. He went to change into his elegant clothes. As he walked down the steps half an hour later, his posture was unnatural, his hand had a slight tremor and his smile was stiff. "I'm not nervous, do I look nervous?" the cousin asked my husband.

"King Solomon, the wisest of all men, always communicated with himself. Throughout *Koheles* King Solomon says, 'I gave to my heart …'; 'I took notice with my heart …'; 'I told my heart to understand …'; 'I said within my heart…' " (*Woman to Woman*, Ch. 5). The skills of inner dialogue can help you achieve a more complete and satisfying life. You will be able to solve practical problems, develop insight into others, improve your relationships, enhance your self-confidence, and reach your goals.

How do you talk to your heart when it seems that your inner self is from a foreign country and can no longer understand plain English? How do you tell your emotions to calm down when you feel intense fear or anger?

When your heart is racing, what will slow it down?

If you are nervous that something might be wrong or that a major life event will soon occur, how can you calm down your stomach *right now*?

What language does the inner you understand?

If you forcibly try to remove negative thoughts about a problem you will often find that the more you try to get rid of the thoughts, the stronger those thoughts become entrenched in your mind (Rabbi Yisrael Salanter).

Does it help to say to yourself, "I should let go of this, because I need to concentrate on other things I must do," or does that just make you feel more restless? It's likely that the events of the day confused your emotions and turned your stomach upside down a few times. Now, although you'd really like to, you can't simply give your mind the order to turn off the voices that attack you. Many people have found that talking directly and logically to themselves and ordering their minds to shut down doesn't work. In fact, it makes things worse. We don't like to follow orders.

Remember the actual responses of the women who reacted to the scenario of their cleaning help canceling the night prior to a big party? Those who pictured a successful outcome to the following day managed better. They made lists to help them visualize how they would do the work themselves, or put on "rollerskates" and began doing something that very moment.

"A person who knows how to direct his inner dialogue in a constructive and positive way can gain tremendous achievement in personality development" (*Rebbetzin Esther Greenberg*). What can specifically be done to control worry in everyday life? The following four steps outline an approach that many have found helpful. Not every person will use every step, but every step should at least be considered. In almost all cases using a combination of steps, depending on time and circumstances, gives the best results.

STEP ONE:
TELL YOUR HEART: THINGS CAN ALWAYS TURN OUT BETTER THAN I EXPECT

Dr. Raymond Abrezol works with athletes and helps them enhance their performance by visualizing success. He says, "The imagination is more powerful than the will. Trying to will away nervousness only adds on more stress to the tension you already have. However, mentally imagining a successful performance in vivid detail liberates the person from unconscious fear" (*Superlearning,* p. 140).

Our hearts find it hard to accept uncertainty. We worry about tomorrow and the changes it will bring. Sometimes we are terrified about tomorrow. How will we manage? There is much that we want to control and we feel helpless because many factors in life are not guaranteed.

Years ago a comment I heard at a lecture by Rebbetzin Bila Kviat hit the bull's-eye. Remembering this idea has given me the impetus to stop and imagine a better outcome whenever my first view of a situation is bleak. Rebbetzin Kviat said, "Every event about which we are in doubt can either succeed or fail. If there are two possibilities, we should logically give a 50 percent prospect to each variable. We tend, however, to expect the worst and worry, although most times things turn out fine. Remember, there is always at least a 50 percent chance that things will be better than you expect."

Do negative thoughts come at you out of nowhere and hit you like a wave? Yes, there is a 50 percent chance that they are justified. Many things can go wrong. Yet there is also at least a 50 percent chance that things can unexpectedly turn out to be better than you think they will be now. You can decide to float on that wave instead of sinking by calmly choosing to imagine a positive outcome.

You can deal effectively with whatever tomorrow brings. Every day is a new beginning. As Rabbi Shlomo Ganzfried says in the *Kitzur Shulchan Aruch:* "The verse, 'They are new every morning how great is Your faithfulness' (*Eichah* 3:23), teaches that every morning a person becomes a new creation."

When my daughter was studying for her Biology midterm she taught me about the miracle of human flexibility and renewal. Did you know that biologically your body has built-in flexibility. Your blood pressure and breathing can fluctuate widely at a moments notice. Every cell and organ can spontaneously adapt to changes in weather, nourishment, and activity. There are dozens of different types of enzymes that your body is creating this very minute. The pattern of electrical firings in your brain is never the same at any given moment in your lifetime. Every minute nearly 300 million cells die, but even more new ones are born in the stream of life that keeps your body functioning.

Every morning a person becomes a new creation.

Chazal said that man is a small world. We can learn many realities about the universe from our bodies. "The continual renewal of things leads man to Hashem — the source of all *phenomena*" (*Sfas Emes, Shabbos Shiurim*). We can trust the wisdom of Hashem that is renewing us daily and providing our bodies with miraculous flexibility to take care of our larger universe as well. We can adapt to tomorrow's challenges with greater ease than we assume. However, tension creates obstacles. Don't add the extra strain of self-imposed pressure.

Deep in the center of you is your *neshamah,* an infinite well of hope, love for Hashem and His children, patience and happiness. Let those feelings flow to the surface. Happy cozy thoughts form a comforting mist around us. We know deep inside that we can find our own success tomorrow in the opportunities presented to us, or at least begin to change our circumstances just a little for the better. Everything we will do can be another step toward achieving Hashem's cosmic goal for us in creation. When we attain our personal optimum we are simultaneously creating positive ripples around us.

Think about each event that will occur tomorrow and form a mental image of your best option. See yourself remaining composed in the doctor's office, passing your driver's test, or having a calm discussion with the boiler repairman. Imagine yourself doing everything right the first time. See yourself with a smile on your face and a relaxed, happy aspect.

This is not just a dream. As Dorothea Brande, editor at the *Chicago Tribune* and *The American Review* in the 1930s said, "Your own success idea is within the region of those things which can be brought about. Usually far from overrating our abilities, we do not understand how great they are."

Exercise: Preparing for Success

We have said that you can prepare for success by imagining yourself doing your best. Right now, let us prepare for success by imagining how well we will do things. In order to discover what to include in our plans we can take a look at our past successes.

a. Describe a time when you felt hopeful and in control of your stress. What was your experience like? What do you think the tranqulity came from?

_____

_____

_____

_____

_____

_____

_____

_____

b. Now write the same experiences in the present tense. Pretend that pleasant day is happening to you right now, *today*.

_____

_____

_____

_____

_____

_____

_____

_____

Throughout the day reread the paragraph you wrote to remind your subconscious mind to cooperate with the new blueprint.

Actual Responses

1. I'm a person who is always involved in different projects that I find challenging, such as baking a unique cake, preparing a motivating lesson, or running a clothing drive for the poor. Since I always make sure that I'm involved in a project, I find that when I am tired or nervous about certain circumstances that are beyond my control it helps to shift my thoughts and focus on my projects. I try to keep in mind the benefits that will accrue to the people I'm help-

ing and the reward for these activities in the World of Truth. If I'm upset, I pick myself up, sort clothes for the clothing drive, knit a special little something for my grandson, or bake a cake for an organization that distributes food to the needy. This agitating time when I can literally drive myself crazy becomes instead an hour of achievement.

2. When I'm feeling tense I take a nice warm shower, pick up an inspiring book or listen for a few minutes to an interesting lecture tape. After that break I am able to be much more productive.

3. Life throws many problems at me that I cannot solve, but on some days I succeed in having a productive day and utilizing the time at hand optimally. When I have had a useful day I fall asleep thinking about how I really spent all my energy working productively. I remember how I spent the day talking in a calm and soft voice and the children responded positively to me and to each other. If I compare the hard days to these days I become aware of a feeling of gratitude.

4. I'll never forget a particular Friday night when I visited a friend. I was dating someone seriously then and I took the weekend off to make a decision. We talked for a while and I aired my conflicting feelings, the good points and the doubts. I felt relieved just to talk about it all. My friend did not give me any answers; she just listened sympathetically. After I finished she told me, "Everyone feels anxious before a decision like this but you do survive the stress. Once you are already engaged all the doubts will disappear and you will just feel this incredible all-encompassing joy." (My friend had recently become engaged herself.)
   Her even disposition and trust flowed into me. I felt secure and peaceful and resolved to take things as they came. It was comfortable. I was in different surroundings from home, kind of on a mini-vacation, and the physical distance helped me feel emotionally removed from all the stresses of the period.

5. Any kind of religious pursuit will help me calm down.

STEP TWO:
TAKE TIME OUT: TO THINK AND FEEL

Frequently, just imagining a successful outcome is enough to help you feel the peace you are craving. You may find, however, that even after visualizing an optimistic result, your mind continues to process the problem.

If the voices in your mind refuse to be silenced it may be a signal that the inner you is lonely for attention. We tend to push ourselves along on one track and are insensitive to the buildup of emotional strain. While pushing away feelings of impending doom seems impossible when we are emotionally tired, once we nourish our psyche we can go on to create a feeling of optimism.

Here are two personal tools that worked best for workshop participants. You can take a physical break from stress by: (a) concentrating on breathing, or (b) nurturing your emotions by caressing nostalgic treasures. Some people like to alternate between the two methods while others prefer settling on one technique which feels the best. Experiment to determine what is most compatible with your personal temperament.

BREATHE EASY

The Midrash says that with each and every breath we take, we should express our gratitude to the A–mighty.

Find a comfortable position, and close your eyes. As you breathe in deeply let the air reach deep inside you and feel the air flow down to your toes. Imagine each breath nourishing your system. Let the air you breathe spread through your face and neck. As you slowly inhale, your arms and hands will feel stronger. Breathe out as slowly as you can with a deep sigh. Now, as you exhale, your arms and hands relax. Allow the tension to drain from your face and feel thankful for each breath. With your eyes still closed, slowly stretch. Listen to the quiet in the room. Sigh and take a few more deep breaths.

How will you know if you are doing this right? Have you ever watched a child sleeping? His stomach goes up and down in a rhythmic wave as he breathes. Put your hand on your stomach area now. You should feel your abdomen push your hand up with each inhalation.

This gives you two benefits. First, your lungs will extract more oxygen with each breath and your blood will be perfectly balanced. Also, concentrating on your breathing will help you banish the tense voices that prevent you from feeling peaceful.

TREASURES ARE A PLEASURE

Think about the week that just passed. You may find that you haven't particularly enjoyed your quieter moments. If we sit back passively the tendency to worry will overwhelm us. I suggest that you prepare a box of nostalgic souvenirs to help chase away negative thoughts.

You cannot think two thoughts at the same time. Consequently when negative thoughts arise, you do not need to fight them. Make an effort to think positive thoughts, and the negative thoughts will disappear (Rabbi Nachman of Breslav).

It's best if you have a really attractive box for your collection of treasures, but in an emergency an ordinary shoe box will do. Gather some small souvenirs of your personal happy times and store them in the box. Ten items is plenty for a beginning, although once you get started you'll find that the box will quickly overflow. Every individual has his own preference. Some people respond to favorite quotations or descriptions in written form, others prefer tapes of music that have special associations for them, while others like to collect pictures. The next time your mind is blank and you hear that inner refrain — "I have nothing to think about" — you will be prepared. Pick up any item in the box. Take a few minutes to really become absorbed in it until you remember something new you hadn't thought of before about your memento. Finally ask yourself, "What is the message from the past that I need right now?"

STEP THREE:
INCREASE YOUR BRAIN POWER:
Listen to tapes for intellectual stimulation.

When your mind races from one idea to the next your pulse and blood pressure tend to rise. If you can focus your thinking by concentrating on something that is intellectually but not emotionally stimulating your brain waves and your system will slow down. Your pulse and blood pressure will even out and your muscles will relax.

The *Sfas Emes* compares the incessant stream of worries to a flood. The concerns of the world and day-to-day survival threaten to drown a person. How can he stay afloat? By constructing a protective ark or vessel. The Hebrew word for ark is *teyvah*. *Teyvah* also means a word. Our words of Torah and prayer help us stay afloat when our material worries overcome us. The *Sfas Emes* teaches a second lesson from the metaphor of Noach's Ark. Just as the Ark needed a light, our words need light if they are to help us stay afloat in life. "Make your words of Torah and prayer glowing and brilliant," the *Sfas Emes* says. "Every word of Torah and Prayer that you express should be brilliant and clear."

Make your words alive. Concentrate when you speak. Your prayer and Torah learning can give you hope that Hashem will help you out of your present darkness.

If you can focus your thinking by concentrating on intellectually stimulating Torah thoughts you will find that apprehension and even physical pain decrease. This technique is so powerful that it has helped people who were ill or in pain relax and fall asleep.

> Ethel's husband was a pediatrician for forty years. After his third heart attack he was told he had a week to live and he left the hospital. He lived for eight wonderful months and left many lovely memories. Jewish tradition emphasizes the importance of visiting the sick, and the congregants of the doctor's *shul* took turns visiting him each day. When a fellow doctor in the neighborhood came, Ethel approached him, "Doctor, please give me something for my husband. He can't sleep at night and he groans in pain. He's keeping me up and I can barely walk around during the day."

Dr. Shuk returned the following day, but his black bag didn't contain the sleeping pills Ethel had expected. "I'm giving you a series of *Daf Yomi* lecture tapes (the daily study of the Talmud)," he said to Ethel's husband. "Tomorrow I'll stop in and we'll talk about everything you heard on the tape. Don't disappoint me."

"This is what carried us through the difficult nights," Ethel declared. "My husband concentrated on Torah learning. His pain abated and he fell asleep peacefully."

Earphones are a wonderful invention. They allow you to listen to tapes without disturbing the peace. Be prepared — don't start rummaging around for tapes at 1 a.m. — and make sure your recorder is working. Many times I've tried my tape recorder to find that the batteries died sometime in the middle of the previous night.

STEP FOUR:
PLAN AHEAD:
Plan ahead for a feeling of accomplishment.

The imagination is a motivating tool that we overlook because we are too busy during the day to daydream. Many times our nervous tension stems from a difficulty in a relationship. It is possible to dream up something good we can do for the person with whom we are dealing. Imagine a successful encounter in vivid detail. This will benefit us immediately. Even at the planning stage we are promised a wonderful reward.

Chazal say that when we cannot sleep at night and we say to ourselves, "Tomorrow when I arise I will do a favor for So-and-so," we will merit to rejoice with the righteous in the World to Come. As it says in *Proverbs* (12:20): וּלְיֹעֲצֵי שָׁלוֹם שִׂמְחָה — "Those who plan to increase peace in the world will merit joy."

Take a few minutes now to plan a kindness you can do for someone tomorrow.

_____

_____

_____

_____

_____

Actual Responses

1. At night I ask myself what I enjoyed doing in the past week or two and picture doing it again. I plan to telephone an elderly neighbor and see if she needs anything. We had a good time when I took her grocery shopping two weeks ago.

2. I'd like to play with my neighbor's children tomorrow so she can have an hour of free time.

3. I'll ask my sister if she wants to go to this workshop next week and give her a ride.

4. I have a few things in mind. I'm going to write letters to my grandchildren; smile at someone I don't particularly care for; and send a get-well card to someone I can't visit.

5. I like to send notes in my children's briefcases along with their lunch so they'll know I think they are pretty wonderful. I also want to bring along pictures the children made for my mother when I visit her.

6. I'm going to visit a friend who slipped on the ice and is homebound and spend some time with her. I bought this nice little dietetic cake that I'm going to bring along.

7. I plan to call two elderly aunts at least once or twice a week. They are both widows.

8. My neighbor's father passed away and her mother is leaving the country this week on a trip. While the girl's mother is away I plan to invite her for supper at least once a week and give her simple recipes that I'll teach her to prepare.

9. I'm going to invite a friend who is divorced to come with her children to dinner and I'll buy something special for her children.

10. It's delicious to fall asleep at night picturing myself being a calm mother. I like to think about getting more organized in the house so everyone will feel cheerful. I'll talk softly and try not to get annoyed too quickly.

11. I'm going to call my aunt overseas tomorrow because it's her birthday. I plan to pop in on my shut-in friend and bring a casserole. I'm also going to keep in touch with my widowed friend even though it's sometimes hard to know what to say.

THE WALL AND THE WIDOW

A wealthy donor heard the Chofetz Chaim's appeal to Polish Jewry on behalf of a proposed new building for the overflowing Yeshivah of Radin. He wanted to provide all of the necessary funds.

"I'm sorry," said the Chofetz Chaim, "but all of Jewry must have a share in building the Yeshivah. The most I can allow you to pay for by yourself is one wall." The rich man paid the 3,000 rubles that he was permitted to give and his name was inscribed on the wall as its donor.

A few years later, during World War I, this supporter died and his estate was confiscated by the government. His widow was left penniless and helpless. The Chofetz Chaim invited her to Radin and gave her an apartment on the Yeshivah grounds. He personally brought her a monthly stipend for her support. Observers couldn't help being awed by the superhuman gratitude of the Chofetz Chaim. They saw a concrete example of "planting charity."

Charity is a seed that bears fruit for its giver too.

Chapter Three
Resisting Insult When Others Are Not Supportive

Mature Joy

by Malky Farkas Treitel

Lasting joy
is not dependent
on external
people
or events.

Instead,
it is a
state
of being
which bubbles
constantly
below
the surface.

So that
even through
sad times
it remains
a healthy
positive
glow
to life.

What happens when your mother calls and although you know she loves you her criticism is hardly loving at all? How do you tell a father or sister or boss or husband who has been insensitive to be more sympathetic and understanding? Most of us feel deep down that we can't change others merely by telling them how we would like them to be. Becoming different takes a long time. It's a rare individual who will listen to another person and agree with their assessment and then immediately begin to change.

STEP ONE: DON'T FOCUS ONLY ON THE INSULT — LOOK AT THE TOTAL PICTURE

Many of us have to face unfair criticism, when people pressure us to do something impossible or disparage our way of doing things. A comment that was uttered in a careless moment may be remembered for many years. How unfortunate that our memory works so well in this specific area.

Rabbi Shaul Katzenellenbogen was a great sage in Vilna. He had an exceptional memory. In his lifetime he never forgot a verse of Torah that he read or heard. His memory was deficient in only one area — if someone insulted him he forgot it immediately (K'tzeis HaShemesh B'Gvuroso p. 153).

It's important not to have an inner tape recorder that repeats negative messages over and over. If we work for a boss who is never satisfied, and he makes us redo our work repeatedly, we begin to say inwardly, "I'm no good." If you don't get the job for which you interviewed, the inner recording says, "You are to blame." This recording talks and talks, giving forth messages like, "If you had been more articulate or worn different clothes the job would be yours." Yet, it is possible that the person who preceded you was hired before you even began your interview.

We can't change other people, but we can react without feeling inadequate or second-rate. Try to hear what the person needs and feels without internalizing the offensive comments that are making their message difficult to accept. People who are nasty are often in distress. We must not let their negativity drag us down.

After a workshop in the neighborhood a participant approached me in tears. "My marriage is breaking up and it's all my fault," she said. She went on to describe that her husband didn't like her cooking, complained that she was overweight, griped about the way she hung up his shirts after she laundered them, and constantly criticized the way she raised the children. "Maybe if I'd done things differently this wouldn't have happened," she whispered. I knew her well and I knew that she is of average weight and very pretty and that she is a loving mother and a skillful cook. I tried to reassure her. "I think your husband's chronic dissatisfaction is a major ingredient here. I think you are a really good person and a talented one. Look at how well you are doing in your career. Look at the many friends you have. We all think you are doing your best. Listen, don't compound the problem by blaming yourself. It's not your fault. It's just not fair for you to accept your husband's negative evaluation without question."

It would surely be best to have Rabbi Katzenellenbogen's talent for forgetting painful comments completely. It helps if we practice looking at the total picture of who we truly are. Each of us has the ability to deal with his or her own pain, fear and loneliness if we can get in touch with who we are. A by-product of this is that we can heal ourselves and by extension others.

In the 1940s Milwaukee had a centennial celebration. It featured a gala week of artistic performances by the country's leading virtuosos. One of them was the operatic tenor, Jan Peerce.

It so happened that the day of Peerce's appearance in Milwaukee was also the day of his father's *yahrzeit*. Peerce consulted the yellow pages, and went to a small synagogue where he asked if he could lead the evening services. He was in great singing form, and the ten men who comprised the *minyan* were treated to a rare performance. Peerce sang every verse of the prayers as an aria.

The following morning Peerce came to the *minyan*, and again turned in a stellar performance. After the services, the synagogue's president, Mr. Goldberg, gave Peerce three dollars. Peerce smiled and graciously refused.

A passerby who recognized Peerce as he left the synagogue went in and asked Goldberg, "What was Jan Peerce doing here?"

Goldberg shrugged his shoulders. "Peerce, shmeerce," he said. "He's a *chazzan* (cantor) who is making the rounds looking for a job for Rosh Hashanah. I wouldn't hire him. He's too loud. Hollers too much."

"Goldberg, you're an idiot," the man said. "That was Jan Peerce, the famous opera singer."

Goldberg appeared unimpressed. He had no idea what opera was nor who Peerce was.

"He's a *chazzan* looking for a position," Goldberg repeated. "I wouldn't take him because he gave me a headache. Besides, with all his singing we wouldn't get out until 5 o'clock. He's not for me. But he tried hard, so I gave him three dollars to help with his expenses. He refused the money; must have been insulted that I didn't give him more. But we are a small synagogue and can't afford to give more. Besides, he's not worth that much more. Hollers too much."

Never in Jan Peerce's illustrious career were any of his critics as harsh on him as Goldberg (*Generation to Generation,* Rabbi Abraham J. Twerski M.D., pp. 235-236).

Jan Peerce was rejected by the president of a minuscule synagogue in Milwaukee. In fact the man didn't have one nice thing to say about him. Do you think Peerce took it personally? Do you think it made any difference to his singing or to his feelings of self-worth and assurance? Probably not. Years of training, practice and performing provide the professional with a cushion that protects him from people who don't appreciate who he is. Perhaps this one person doesn't understand but there are hundreds of others who know his value.

However, if we aren't professionals but just ordinary people who are constantly facing changes and trying to perfect ourselves, doubt does tend to plague us at times.

STEP TWO:
SURROUND YOURSELF WITH
SUPPORTIVE PEOPLE

It's a lamentable truth that many of us have to deal with some irrational people. It's sad when those who are closest to us can't give us the understanding and assurance we need. How can we help ourselves ? Our best option is to accept this fact with grace and flexibility and not become consumed by conflict. Instead, we should reach out and find strength from other people we know.

It is often difficult to find the supportive people in our lives because we are looking in the wrong place. We expend our energy on achieving closeness with the people we think we should impress. Rather, we should seek out those who are already close to us. Look to the people who see things as you do. They may not dress fashionably, but they are cheerful and easygoing. Someone you can help and who has similar interests may be waiting for you to begin a mutually beneficial relationship. Don't push people away because they are too young or too old. Often, older people have more time and more wisdom. Finally, realize that it's fine to ask for help in addition to offering your assistance.

Why is it important to connect with people who affirm and respect us? Having supportive people around us not only improves the quality of life, it actually extends life. Dr. David Spiegel conducted a study involving a group of women with recurrent breast cancer. He organized a group of women who were dealing with similar trials. He discovered that the average length of life for the women who, in addition to their treatment, participated in a support group, was double that of the women who received only mainstream medicine. [David Spiegel M.D. is Professor of Psychiatry and Behavioral Sciences and Director of the Psychosocial Treatment Laboratory at Stanford University School of Medicine] (*Healing and the Mind*, Bill Moyers, p. 331).

Where can you meet new people ? One place to find friends is at a Torah class. (You are invited to the one in my home.)

The women who attend my class have become a unit — a group of friends who help one another. At my workshops although everyone comes expecting to learn from me, actually much more occurs. The participants in the group teach each other and teach me. We each have a very deep wisdom that is unique to us. It's not found in books or in schools. It's found in life.

Exercise: To Whom Do You Turn for Support?

_____

_____

_____

_____

Actual Responses

1. I turn to young children for support. Young children always remind me that I'm special just as I am. There is a beautiful innocence to their genuine affection. They accept you just as you are and respond to your attempts at conversation, song or smiles with sincere excitement. Whatever they do is like a miracle.

2. I turn to Hashem for support — I felt overwhelmed, there were so many things to take care of that I acquired a worried state of mind. Finally I said," Master of the Universe, I can't worry anymore! I can't deal with all this. I'm giving it over to You." I felt so unburdened afterwards. It was excellent. Now I don't even remember what the problem was anymore. Hashem took care of it for me.

3. The people in our _shul_ are very supportive. My husband was out of a job. He met someone in shul and told him his problem. An hour later this person called from the

yeshivah. "We had to dismiss one of our workers. I just checked with the administrator and he said you should come for an interview." My husband is still working there five years later.

4. I turn to people at this class for support. I was looking for work. I was willing to volunteer to teach English to Russian immigrants because I wanted to keep busy. I was planning to go to my old workplace and get a list of potential students. Then at the class last week I met Esther. Esther told me she's tutoring at Touro and gave me the number to call. You see I'm dressed spiffy today. Well, I just came back from the interview and I got the job at Touro!

TURN TO HASHEM FOR SUPPORT

Excerpt from *Grandma* — a biography of Mrs. Devorah Sternbuch:

Once when Reb Elchonon Wasserman was visiting the family, Grandma asked him to *bentch* the children. He blessed them that they should be Torah scholars. She interjected, "This isn't enough. There are Torah Scholars who don't have fear of Heaven."Reb Elchonon added, "Indeed they should have fear of Heaven too." She continued, "What about a *berachah* for myself?" Reb Elchonon replied, "If you have children who are Torah scholars and have fear of Heaven and they give you *nachas*, this is the greatest blessing." But she was not satisfied. "No," she declared. "I need a blessing that the A–mighty should have *nachas* from me." Reb Elchonon immediately acceded to her request.

Grandma once told one of her grandchildren that when she became a widow, there were so many things to ask from Hashem that she didn't know where to begin. "Finally I decided to pray that He have *nachas* from my children. I knew that if they bring Him *nachas*, then I will have *nachas* too."

STEP THREE:
FORGIVE OTHERS AND JUDGE YOUR PEERS FAVORABLY

The supportive people around us can help us put criticism into perspective. The next step to healing our emotional hurts is forgiving others. There is a basic principle in Rabbinic literature: בְּמִדָּה שֶׁאָדָם מוֹדֵד בָּהּ מוֹדְדִין לוֹ, "By the yardstick that a man measures others will he himself be measured" (*Sotah* 8b). Hence, he who refuses to forgive others when insulted could hardly expect to be forgiven by Heaven for his transgressions. Similarly, he who judges his fellow man charitably could hopefully expect to be judged similarly himself.

Once the Baal Shem Tov *zt"l* was sitting with his *chassidim*. A poor ignorant man entered. The Baal Shem immediately called him to the head of the table and seated the man beside him. Astonished, the disciples asked why he accorded this honor to an unknown ignorant person in tattered garments. Surely he did not belong at the head of the table!

The Baal Shem replied, "In the World to Come I too will want a 'seat' near the head, and I will certainly be asked through what merit I deserve it. The only answer I will have will be that at one time I took a poor man without grace or learning and gave him a seat of honor."

THE OTHER SIDE OF THE COIN

Whenever we discuss forgiving others the static crackles in the room. People have very strong feelings on this topic. At the beginning of one class Gitty described her struggle with this issue.

"One summer when I was a young girl in camp, I had a bitter fight with a close friend and confidant. She gossiped about me to make herself look good. This caused me great distress. When I was approached by a third party to forgive her, I immediately said yes. We tried to mend our friendship, but it was never the same again. It is very easy to mouth the words, 'I am sorry' and it is just as easy to answer, 'Yes, I accept your apology,' but to really continue as if the hurt was not there is a difficult task. Once I was hurt, I found it hard to trust this friend again."

Gitty thought for a moment and then added, "When we make a mistake we would like to be forgiven automatically, because we mouth the words 'I am sorry.' We should realize that the person who was hurt may want to forgive but their pain is too great."

Hurt feelings tend to linger. Critical words that were aimed at us, repeated requests that were ignored, promises not kept — all these scenes replay in our minds in vivid color. How do we erase those images? We understand that it is important to forgive, yet it is difficult to do so. As Rabbi Moshe Chaim Luzzatto says in *Mesillas Yesharim,* "Forgiving and forgetting an insult is easy for the heavenly angels."

Does our anger help us at all? When we hold onto our hurt we experience the sadness all over again. Does speaking to others in an angry tone help? "Anger is good for nothing," said the popular psychologist Dr. Wayne W. Dyer. When you are angry you can't communicate well with anyone. Self-control is so important that the successful CEO of AVIS Rent-A-Car advises that when you are angry you should, "Tell those you are meeting with that you have a phone call and leave the room for a few minutes. When you are alone concentrate on your goals and ask yourself what you really want to accomplish."

How do we overcome our natural tendency to hold onto our hurt feelings?

"A distinguished scholar by the name of Rav Tzvi Genot lived in Jerusalem. After he passed away, papers recounting many interesting experiences were found among his effects. He wrote that once someone had insulted him. Although he did not answer, he felt slighted. He was troubled that he should have ill feelings against the person who made the remark. To dispel such feelings, he would try to find virtues in this person. He bought a small notebook in which he recorded two virtues each day, and in less than a month he found he had recorded over fifty virtues. With the realization of what a fine individual this person must be, his grudge simply melted away" (A *Twist of The Tongue*, Rabbi M. Oppen, p. 81).

After one of my workshops Seryl tried the exercise above. Her experience encouraged us all to use this technique to put together the ingredients of a renewed relationship. Here is her story:

"One of our Shabbos guests came by late on Friday afternoon when I was bathing my son and I couldn't come to the door. He said, 'Can I have a pot? I need a pot tonight.' My husband grabbed a pot from the counter and gave it to him. When I came down I discovered that my guest had borrowed one of my best pots, one that had cost around $60.

"I waited for him to return the pot. I didn't want to insist, for perhaps he needed it. Every week when cooking for Shabbos, I had to cook in shifts because of the missing pot. One evening, after two and a half months, our guest returned the pot.

" 'By the way,' said the guest offhandedly, 'I guess I shouldn't have put your pot in the oven, the handles kind of melted.'

"I tried to remain calm. I said in a low voice. 'How can you ruin a pot by putting it in the oven? No one can use it anymore. Please don't borrow our things from now on. I needed this pot. It will be expensive to replace. Why did you keep it for so long?'

" 'Look here,' the guest replied. 'It's not my fault. You should have called and asked for it. As for the misshapen handles, well, no one warned me about that. Anyhow the pot still works. I guess if you don't want me I won't come for Sabbath lunch this week,' he concluded.

"At first I thought that maybe some peace and quiet would be nice for a change. But I didn't feel that peace and quiet. I realized that I'm the one struggling with bitter and resentful feelings. My guest just doesn't understand how a woman wants the pots in her kitchen to look.

"I decided to force myself to follow the exercise we learned and find two good things about my guest. I was not in the mood to stop the blaming, but I told myself to change my focus for 15 minutes. Every person has at least two good qualities. The first good thing I thought of was that he has a terrific rapport with my four children. He knows how to play with them and how to tell stories. The second good thing was that he does try to be a gentleman. Two or three times a year he buys useful appliances for the house or large bouquets of flowers to show his appreciation.

"That first seed of charitable thinking led me to realize that I really didn't want this guest to stop coming. The kids adore him and I know they will repeatedly ask me what happened to him.

"I called back. I said that I had thought it over and realized that I had been too critical. Perhaps what happened was an innocent mistake. We made peace. I felt I was back on track and going in the right direction again."

Exercise

Now it's your turn. I hope that you will want to incorporate this idea into your daily routine and that you will buy your own little notebook for recording the virtues of your family and close friends. In the meantime, the best way to start is by attempting the method right now. So in the lines below briefly record a mildly upsetting incident with someone you know. Then write down two good qualities that person has.

Since this is a new idea and forgiving others is a skill we have to develop, start out with only a mildly upsetting incident that you know you can feel gracious about.

_____

_____

_____

_____

_____

_____

Actual Responses

1. My brother-in-law spoke rudely to me. My first thought was to stew in anger and escalate this into a full scale quarrel. Two good things —
   a. He does favors for lots of people and has done favors for us.
   b. He works hard for his children's school.

2. My teenage daughter loves nice dresses and other objects that are all very expensive! She nags and nags me to buy them for her.
   a. She's very helpful.
   b. She is really very giving when she doesn't have hours of homework.

3. My father-in-law was taking me and my three little boys to New Jersey. One of the boys touched something in the car that upset him. He yelled and said some hurtful things. Right away I thought —
   a. He really is helping us by giving us this ride.
   b. Maybe something happened to him that got him upset. (Sure enough I found out that as he was coming to pick us up some punk came up to the window while he was waiting at the red light, punched him in the face and called him a bad name.)

4. A relative made me feel bad by not sharing in helping with the annual family get-together.
   a. She's very neat and keeps a spotless home.
   b. She's soft-spoken and gentle in her manner.

5. My son tried to throw out a lot of my precious stuff when I was moving and I got really nervous and upset.
   a. He helps me whenever he can.
   b. He really has my good in mind.

6. When I was moving I gave away a piece of furniture to my Russian housekeeper. It was something that a good friend

once owned. Now after many years she wants it back. My friend is unfairly upset with me.
a. She tries to be consistently helpful.
b. She is a sincere friend.

7. The teacher gave my child a C+ in conduct.
   a. She tells interesting stories to benefit the class.
   b. She gives fair tests and my child's average is 10 points higher than last year.

We discussed three practical methods in this chapter. First — make a realistic inventory of your strengths. Try to see the bigger picture instead of focusing on the unpleasantness of the insult. Second — reach out to a supportive person who can give you comfort and strength. Third — forgive, by looking for good traits in the person who hurt your feelings.

All of these techniques can help you improve your life. However, it's important to know what to change and why to change. Struggling to change your behavior is much more difficult if it is not based on self-esteem. We should strive to modify the essential things, not the trivial incidentals that may impress others. Real change must be motivated by strength and self-appreciation in order for it to last. In this interview Charna describes her intense struggle to accept and value herself according to **her** ideals, despite failing to impress a pretentious individual.

Interview

Roiza: Sometimes one is in an embarrassing situation and it's necessary to take courage by remembering our innate worth. Has this ever happened to you?

Charna: When I was married for about two years, I tried to get involved with a charitable organization. They were planning a tea and I volunteered to sell raffles at the front door. They requested that everyone come dressed formally because they wanted to make a nice impression. When I arrived the president of the organization said, "We asked that you wear a formal outfit." "These are my dressier clothes," I replied.

Roiza: What happened next?

Charna: When I got home I discussed the incident with my husband because I did feel resentful and embarrassed. He said, "You are great just the way you are." His words took the hurt away. He also said that I should be above all this — one's character is what counts. Today, three years later, I feel more confident and comfortable being myself. Experience has helped. When I wake up in the morning I know who I am and what I am supposed to do and that gives me self assurance.

Roiza: How did you learn about this value? Is there someone you admire who has a lot of self-respect?

Charna: Listening to Rabbi Avigdor Miller's manner of handling challenging questions has given me a feeling of inner strength. He isn't afraid to take a stand on controversial issues. If someone asks a question about something that the Torah forbids he will openly say, "This topic is not debatable." He's always polite and sometimes exhibits a refreshing sense of humor, but he's firm at the same time.

Roiza: How can other people feel comfortable facing disapproval?

Charna: If you are strong in your beliefs, your beliefs will outweigh the doubts that are caused by critics. It also helps to find others who are swimming against the current. My friends help me remember what is really appropriate when society pressures us say-ing, "Don't be so square, it's fine to do, to be or to want ..."

Roiza: What methods have helped you handle insults?

Charna: I use one of three approaches and sometimes all of them.
1. Let this be an atonement for something I've done wrong.
2. Know who is saying the insult — even if they are on par with me they have no right to insult me.
3. I go through my mental list of people less fortunate than me to whom I can be more caring and sensitive. The pain of the insult reminds me not to look down on others.

CHAPTER FOUR

Sunshine, Rain and Words

The Rabbis have taught: When R' Eliezer was ill, four Elders came to visit him, R' Tarfon, R' Yehoshua, R' Elazar ben Azaryah and R' Akiva. R' Tarfon said, "You are more valuable to *Klal Yisrael* than the drops of rain, for rain is precious in this world while a teacher is both in this world and in the World to Come." R' Yehoshua said, "You are more valuable to *Klal Yisrael* than the sun. The sun gives benefit in this world while a teacher is both in this world and in the World to Come ..." (*Sanhedrin* 101a).

Each one of the disciples elucidated another component of the *talmid-rebbi* relationship. R' Tarfon indicated the impetus for growth which the teacher imparts to the student, comparing it to the rain's benefit on the seedling. The soul of a person embedded in his body is very much a dormant seedling waiting for the "rain" to cause it to sprout. Without an external force to awaken it, it remains inanimate, blossoming forth only due to the inspiration of the teacher (*Reb Chaim's Discourses,* p. 268).

Deep within our hearts lie many seeds. In the dark recesses of the subconscious, dreams and aspirations are entombed. A small voice whispers "perhaps ...," but the rushing waves of routine life shout — "No!" The tiny kernel of hope thirsts for a paltry droplet of encouragement. A smile of sunshine and the refreshing trickle of kind words can sustain a dream and make it grow.

Although there are many marvelous ways you can help others, dispensing encouraging words is different because it's easily accessible. Every kind word sprouts warm feelings. Supportive words are a catalyst for growth. A compliment can call forth images and possibilities. Your thoughtful reassurance can encourage someone on the expressway to their dreams. Decide to assist family, friends and even strangers by dispensing good words wherever you go. Good words, like rain, generate growth quietly, in the subconscious. The belief in one's competence is a root that eventually bears abundant produce.

I learned about personal growth from potatoes. What does a potato have to do with words, hopes and dreams? When you plant one potato you get ten times as many. When you plant good words you also reap a fruitful crop. Friendship, good feelings, health and hope grow from good words. My friend Peninah described the phenomenon of growth.

Peninah teaches kindergarten. One day she brought in a potato, a large pot and some earth. As the class watched, she took the potato, cut it into four pieces and planted it. Afterwards she covered the potato pieces with earth. Every day a different student maneuvered the pot into the sunlight and carefully watered it. Five weeks later, Peninah asked her four-year-old students, "How many potatoes did I put in the pot?" "One!" they replied. "How many potatoes are in the pot now?" Peninah asked. "One!" the girls all said with a giggle.

"Look carefully, now," Peninah announced cheerfully. The girls crowded around a table in the center of the room as Peninah began to dig in the container. She pulled out one potato and then two. The girls exclaimed and laughed. Peninah continued digging. She pulled out a third potato and then a fourth. By now, the four-year-olds were jumping up and down. Smiling, Peninah clarified, "This is how our food grows from a seed. We put in only one potato and some dirt but each piece grew into a whole new potato. We could have had ten potatoes if we would have had a bigger pot. That's the miracle of growth. Hashem makes all our food grow just like this."

Peninah's description of the delight and surprise of her young students at finding so many potatoes inspired me. I say a good word and nurture a seed in someone's soul. I go on with my life but secretly the seed of hope is growing in someone's consciousness. Perhaps they will remember and repeat my words when they feel self-doubt. Words are small yet powerful. Words grow into accomplishments.

Seven words have changed my life. They are, "With Hashem's help, you can do it!" These words, like rain, nourished a seed inside me, producing a beautiful yield. When I was in ninth grade I was anxious because I had never taken mid-terms before. My sister said, "You can do it. You have always done well on tests." When I was in 11th grade and I was asked to speak for 150 fellow students, my favorite teacher, Rebbetzin Malka Paretzky, said, "With Hashem's help, you can do it. Just remember to look at the audience when you speak. They don't care if your words are perfect. They want you."

Eight years ago, my aunt, who is an English professor, said, "Since you give so many lectures you should write a book." I said, "I have several years of speaking experience but I don't know if I can write a book. I never had a knack for writing." My aunt said, "You can do it. You already have the ideas and that's half the job." A year later, I gave my aunt a brown manila envelope. It contained the manuscript of my first book. She read it and said, "With Hashem's help you can do it. Publish it! Your next books will be even better."

The dew moistens the earth, and a bulb, withered and dry, becomes a flower. One potato grows into ten. An apple pit grows into a tree. What growth do words nourish? You won't know until you begin planting them. I wrote this poem to help me plant words; it is for you, dear reader. Enjoy it and share it with others.

YOU CAN DO IT!

Sitting down for a rest,
thinking about the people
I like best.

WHY?

Because you strive to grow,
you have goals and dreams.
And from them
the blessing flows.

Sitting down for a rest,
thinking about you,
admiring your zest.

You cross your oceans,
you build your bridges.
When you fail
you rise again.

WHAT?

What did I want to tell you?

With Hashem's guiding Hand
You Can Do It!
I Know you will find a way.

With Hashem's guiding Hand
You Can Do It!
Just decide to start today.

When you succeed
please let me know, please do!
Because I'll want to celebrate with you.

The seeds of possibility in the human soul need sunshine and rain. Good words are the rain and a smile is the sunshine. Rabbi Yehoshua said that Rabbi Eliezer was like the smiling sun. A teacher illuminates his students' path in life, and causes them to grow and mature.

Chazal say that everyone yearns for Hashem's smile — if Hashem will smile on us we will enjoy the sunshine of good fortune. How can we merit Hashem's smile? When we illuminate our friend's path with a smile, Hashem smiles down upon us.

In daily life there are so many wonderful opportunities to smile. We think we don't have time to stop and smile so we remain gray and gloomy inside. If only we would smile, the joy would penetrate our hearts. A smile brings you much closer to others and to Hashem.

We hesitate to smile upon those who probably need it most. Someone who is suffering often remains alone simply because people think that they somehow will fail to provide comfort and won't "do it right." Ask yourself instead, "Why shouldn't I try?"

Usually the fear is worse than the actual reality. Quite often we do succeed in motivating and encouraging others. Often life can be very surprising. We can actually change a life with a few caring moments.

Do you have a ready smile? Do you believe that people are basically good? Are you sensitive to their emotions? Do people feel good around you? Are you interested in learning from others?

If you can answer yes to these questions, then you are ready to reach out more often to others. Everyone walks about with a destination in mind but some people create beautiful scenes in the hearts of the people they encounter along the way. Endow caring surprises upon others and Hashem will bestow more and more wonderful surprises upon you.

You have a bigger impact than you think you do and everyone benefits. Everyone gets ahead. It really is like that.

Exercise: Smile Break

Don't let any good thing that happens to you just pass you by without your being aware of it. Your problems are not an excuse to stop living. Concentrate on the good. Savor the sunshine. Notice the flowers. Ponder the clouds sailing in the sky. Take a "smile break."

A smile break is better than a coffee break. Coffee has caffeine and the cake that you eat with the coffee may be unhealthy … A smile break is good for you spiritually, emotionally and physically. A few times a day just stop everything, sit down, smile and say *Modeh Ani*. I thank you Hashem right now because …

WILL YOU DO IT RIGHT NOW?

Right now let's pause for a minute and smile. Let's think how happy we are simply to be alive. Smiling leads to grateful thoughts. Jot down three grateful thoughts that came to your mind now while you were smiling.

I'm smiling now because :

1. _____

2. _____

3. _____

Try to take a "smile break" a few times a day.

Actual Responses

1. a. My family is in good health.
    b. The hand I sprained in a fall a month ago feels better.
    c. My friend's daughter is getting married in a month.

2. a. The sun is shining.
    b. This workshop is fun.
    c. I'm alive and well.

3. a. My eyelashes keep out the dust and make me look beautiful.
    b. My lungs inhale and exhale without any effort.
    c. It's rose-fever season but this year I'm taking garlic and vitamin C and it has helped me feel great.

4. a. Today I talked to my sister who lives out of town.
    b. I went out of the way to pick someone up.
    c. I said the bedtime *Shema* with concentration last night and I think it made today flow more smoothly.

Chapter Five
Twelve Quick Tips to Help You Manage Stress

One can never have enough tips for dealing with stress. These tips have already been presented in the context of the previous chapters. However, when you need a quick reference and reminder this chapter will be your guide.

These tips are intended to be practical. They should work. If they don't work the first time you try don't give up. Remember, optimally our energy is used not by wasting it on unproductive stress, but by utilizing it to further our inner growth and strengthen family and friends.

1. **RECOGNIZE WORRY AS THE YETZER HARA'S VOICE —** Moshe Chaim Luzzatto, author of *Mesillas Yesharim* says, "This is one of the clever devices of the evil inclination — to mount constant pressure on the hearts and minds of men until they don't have a calm moment to consider and observe the type of life they are leading." There is a constant dialogue in our heart and mind. There is an incessant stream of thoughts, yearnings, and cravings. The evil inclination confuses us with incessant chatter so that we cannot adequately discharge our responsibilities (Chapter One).

2. **DON'T ADD TO YOUR STRESS BY THINKING — "I'M THE ONLY ONE"** — Sima said, "When I was in the third grade a professional assessment team was sent to our school to check everyone's eyesight and hearing. I stood in front of the room and couldn't see the eye chart. The nurse wrote the following note to my mother, 'Your daughter cannot read.' All day I worried about this note. How could I show my mother a note that says I can't read? I'm in the third grade. I must be the only third grader with this problem. When I came home my mother laughed and said, 'Don't worry. We'll get you an appointment with the eye doctor for glasses.' The solution was so obvious and so simple."

Some of us are better at hiding it, but it is human nature to feel pressured. Stress consumes our time and energy. We add to its effects by isolating ourselves. Do you remember how many of your worries as a child seemed unsolvable because you were ashamed to talk about them ? Once you mustered the courage to speak, you realized that your problem could be tackled.

Real problems are serious enough. Don't add to them by isolating yourself. If you aren't sure of the facts, inquire and get a clear picture (Chapter One).

3. **OPTIMISTIC OUTLOOK** — Think about each event that will occur tomorrow and form a mental image of your best option. Consider all the situations you will encounter and how they can best be handled. What words will you use? What tone of voice is best? The right words can help you get through your day with less stress and fatigue. With the extra energy you may wish to work on actualizing a secret dream.

4. **TAKE TIME OUT TO THINK AND FEEL** — It is utterly illogical. In order to accomplish our goals we drive ourselves relentlessly. If we would only take opportunities for short breaks we would accomplish more and save our emotional and physical health. Specific tools to try are in Chapter Two — *Breathe Easy* and *Treasures are a Pleasure.*

5. **INCREASE YOUR BRAIN POWER** — Listen to Torah tapes for intellectual stimulation. Rabbi Ezriel Tauber often quotes the

Rambam's saying, "According to one's knowledge of Hashem, one's love of Hashem intensifies." Rabbi Tauber explains, "Every time you listen to a Torah tape you are performing the *mitzvah* of *Ve'ahavta es Hashem Elokecha.*"

6. **PLAN TO DO AN ACT OF KINDNESS TOMORROW** — *Chazal* say that when we cannot sleep at night and we say to ourselves, "Tomorrow when I arise I will do a favor for So-and-so," we will merit to rejoice with the righteous in the World to Come. As it says in *Proverbs*, "*Ul'yo'atzei shalom simchah* — Those who plan to increase peace in the world will merit joy."

7. **DON'T FOCUS ONLY ON THE INSULT — LOOK AT THE TOTAL PICTURE** — Many of us have to face unfair criticism when people pressure us to do something impossible or disparage our way of doing things. A comment that was uttered in a careless moment may be remembered for many years. How unfortunate that our memory works so well in just this area. When an insult bothers you, sit down and make a list of five compliments you have heard in the past (Chapter Three).

8. **THINKING OF OTHERS IS REFRESHING** — One way to connect with others is by being truly interested in them. Try to talk for 15 minutes a day without using the words I, me, my, mine. This practice allows you to see yourself in perspective. Stop focusing on your own problems. By concentrating your attention on others you will gain a refreshing outlook on your own life.

9. **SURROUND YOURSELF WITH SUPPORTIVE PEOPLE** — When you decide to share a problem be selective. Seek out someone who has a talent for seeing the good in others and in you (Chapter Three, pp. 44-46).

10. **FORGIVE OTHERS AND IMPROVE A RELATIONSHIP BY LOOKING FOR THE GOOD** — Write a letter in which you focus on the good qualities of someone in your family. Simply

look for aspects or activities which can be honestly reported in a positive way. There is good in everyone.

11. **TAKE A SMILE BREAK** — Sit down and smile for a few minutes. Write down three things you can be grateful for right now (Chapter Four).

12. **PLANT ENCOURAGING WORDS** — Pause on the threshold of any crowded room you are about to enter and consider how you can encourage a few people in that room. At a *chasunah,* notice not only the *kallah* and her mother but also the grandmother, great-aunt and younger sister. In the classroom don't compliment only the teacher; remember that the assistant teacher is probably working at least as hard. The *frum* cashier in the grocery who is working at 2:30 on *Erev Shabbos* could use an encouraging word. Finally, you don't have to be the rebbetzin to notice a newcomer in *shul* and welcome them to the neighborhood.

Words
Habits
Actions
Thoughts

Chapter Six
Decisions: Making Better Choices

Reb Aryeh Levin *zt"l* said, "We are commanded, וּבָחַרְתָּ בַּחַיִּים, to choose life. Why does Hashem give us such a command? After all, isn't this something everyone decides to do? Don't we all struggle to survive? Wouldn't we all sacrifice everything we have to acquire life and health? Rav Aryeh concluded, "If we look closely at the words, a more precise interpretation would be *choose* in life, because there is life and then THERE IS LIFE."

Living doesn't mean simply not dying. We all must resolve to live a life of purpose. Decide to advance yourself and achieve more. Decide wisely. Choose an eternal life by making each action you perform elevated and noble. It all begins with you.

It is your responsibility to make decisions about what you will and will not do. Sometimes people say, "If my family were different or my friends were more supportive I'd make better choices." You cannot blame others for your choices. Don't use your energy to change others. Instead, use that same energy to clarify your choices and to take new actions on your behalf.

When we focus on trying to change others it creates problems that grow like mushrooms: headaches, chronic bitterness and fatigue, to name just a few. However, when we focus on making ourselves stronger and improving our behavior many benefits blossom, such as: energy, confidence and courage.

In the parable that follows the Chofetz Chaim demonstrates that although we cannot directly piece together the entire world, we can improve the world when we take charge of our time, our days and our lives.

Yaakov woke up on a rainy Sunday morning. He looked out the window and watched the streams of water running down the pane. He drew pictures on the misty glass. Yaakov watched the cars with their oscillating windshield wipers drive past. "I wish we could go out," he thought.

Yaakov ran to his mother. "Mommy I really want to put on my raincoat and go for a walk. I'm bored."

Yaakov's mother took a deep breath. No! She didn't want to go for a walk right now. She searched desperately in her mind for something her son might like to do. Would he want to look at the new magazine that was on the table? She began leafing through the pages. Yaakov's mother noticed a map of the world.

"Look Yaakov," she called. "I found something that will be lots of fun. I'll make you a puzzle out of this map."

Yaakov's mother carefully cut the map into 50 small pieces and put them into a ziploc bag. "Now you have a new puzzle. You can put together the whole world."

Yaakov enthusiastically, sifted through the pieces. He found three that matched and made up the United States but then the puzzle began to get difficult. Where was Zambia? Was it in South America or in Africa? Where did Greenland go? Did it go on the top or on the bottom. "It looked so easy but I just can't do it," Yaakov thought. "How am I supposed to put the whole world together?" Yaakov took a handful of pieces and tossed them aimlessly into the air. A few pieces fell upside down. Yaakov stared at them and thought he recognized something familiar. "Could it be what I think it is?" Yaakov murmured.

Yaakov flipped over the pieces. "Let's see now," he thought. "Here's an eye and this is part of a nose. That other piece resembles a fingertip." Now Yaakov was ecstatic. He may not know all the countries in Africa but he knew what a boy like himself looked like.

After fifteen minutes the puzzle was finished. It was a picture of a boy learning from a *Chumash*. He got out some scotch tape and secured the pieces together. Now he could turn it over to the other side.

"Come Mommy!" Yaakov called, "I just put together the world."

"Yaakov, that's marvelous," the mother replied. "How did you complete the puzzle so quickly?"

Yaakov smiled. "I noticed there was a picture of a boy on the other side. When I put the boy together, the world came together" (based on a Parable by the Chofetz Chaim).

We often think that if we can change the world around us then we will be happy. Like the boy trying to figure out where to put Madagascar, we work ceaselessly to solve problems in our larger universe. We make an unpleasant situation unworkable by telling ourselves, "I will be happier when my situation improves." We continually use the phrase "if only" in our inner dialogue: "If only I got more sleep at night; if only Esther would return my call; if only I lived somewhere else; if only my parents, brothers and sisters were more understanding; if only the Chanukah party were over (I should never have volunteered to help out) — then I'd be happy."

On the other side of the puzzle is the picture of the boy. We do not have to wait passively for circumstances to change in order to be happier. *We can be happier right now by taking responsibility for our attitudes and our spirituality.* The question, "How can we put together a better identity?" is a vital one because if we can improve ourselves we can change the world.

As Rabbi Moshe Chaim Luzzatto says in *Mesillas Yesharim* (Ch. 1, 21): *"If you look more deeply into the matter, you will see that the world was created for man's use. In truth, man is the center of a great balance. If he is pulled after the world and is drawn further from his Creator, he is damaged and he damages the world with him. If he rules over himself and unites himself with his Creator, and uses the world only to aid him in the service of his Creator, he is uplifted and the world itself is uplifted with him."*

Why is it that although we have the best intentions our plans for self-improvement quickly evaporate after a day or two without any measurable progress? After Yom Kippur we feel awful that one-fourth of our confessions were about sins relating to speech, so we resolve never to speak *lashon hara*. We realize that

Minchah is an important prayer and there is no excuse because it only takes a few minutes, so we decide to *daven Minchah* from today on. We hear a lecture about communicating with children and decide that we will never scream or threaten again. The goal of "be perfect" usually ends up in "do nothing."

Many intricate aspirations loom large and overwhelming. They become manageable when the steps are made practicable. If you find yourself avoiding some task that you want to tackle or ignoring a goal that you want to pursue, your problem may be that your first step is too complicated. Break it down. Continue your task reduction until your first step is one that you can manage without dread. Don't underestimate the power of small steps.

The first small success will lead to further progress. Consider how you might apply the "small step principle" to cleaning the house, being vigilant about your speech, or being calm with your children.

In regard to cleaning the house, if "clean the basement" was your first step you probably didn't make your first step small enough. Filling up one bag of things to give away might be a better and more attainable step. Deciding you won't ever speak slander is wonderful but it might work better if you resolve to be careful about your speech every morning for one hour. The goal of always being calm with the children might ironically make you feel like a pressure cooker about to explode. Perhaps if you aim to start the day off by being cheerful in the morning you can advance further.

Small steps gently lead even the most reluctant among us to triumph in our personal growth. Usually a brief victory will be enough to motivate us and more will be accomplished than the small step would indicate.

A different way to take a small but significant first step is suggested by Rabbeinu Yonah in the *sefer Shaarei Teshuvah. Decide to be 100 percent the best you can be for a short period of time. In the morning decide to aim high from the time you wake up until breakfast. Then set a new objective from breakfast to lunch and begin again from lunch until supper.*

There are many possibilities in life. When pondering your choices and trying to make a better decision, it's important to remember that many things that seem impossible are not. If you do them once. they become more attainable.

When I studied in Seminary in *Eretz Yisrael,* everyone felt nervous about having a private audience with the principal. Perhaps it was because we revered her so much and she demanded intense inner scrutiny and honesty; therefore meeting with her meant meeting with our innermost selves. At the first class I resolved to give this year of study my utmost effort. I listened to every word and took careful notes. I pondered impossible homework questions each night and sometimes arrived at the correct answer. I longed to have a personal interview with the principal. However, I couldn't do it. I thought it was impossible. About a month into the school year the Rebbetzin extended an invitation at least once a week, "If anyone has any questions I'd be happy to make up a time when we can discuss things," or "I have some fascinating material on this subject in my library. It would be my pleasure to have some of you come over to read it in my home."

I looked around the classroom. Out of eighty students one hand would go up and it wasn't mine. No, It's impossible. I can't do it. What will I say? How can I be sure I won't make a mistake? I'll probably say something silly. I wanted so much to go. I admired my principal's joy in Torah, her enthusiasm and energy. I admired her depth of wisdom. I wanted to ask so many burning questions.

We had another teacher who was easy to approach. She baked *challah* with us, invited us to her house when we got sick, and even went on a tour of Eilat with us. Once after class I came up to ask a question. She look directly at me and said, "That's a question for the Rebbetzin." It was impossible to say no to her so I said, "Yes, I will go and speak with the Rebbetzin." Once I went it was no longer impossible. I had many opportunities to talk with the Rebbetzin after that. Those conversations changed my life.

Every morning you face the most important moment of your day. It takes only a minute to decide to give today your best talents, your best energy, and your best attitude. It takes only a moment to decide to savor all you have. Today you can choose to enjoy your vision, the ability to stand erect, and your freedom to move about. Resolve today to enjoy the people around you whom you love.

Some of our most important decisions are often determined by others. Does someone's look or derisive laughter or snide remark really have to ruin our day? Does someone's indifference have to constrict our true shining soul, like a cloud blocks the sun?

Decide for today and for this week what little victories can mean the difference between giving up and hoping that things will get better. When you feel like quitting what can you choose to do to motivate your inner self? Set a goal and plan to achieve it. You can only build up momentum if you begin the task.

Decide to be the best you can be. Decide to dream. Decide to achieve. Your experiences depend on your choices. Remember Rav Aryeh Levin's words, "There is life and there is LIFE." Choose LIFE.

Exercise

MAKING DECISIONS AND ACTING UPON THEM				
DECISION Write your decision clearly.	**METHOD** What must you do?	**ASSETS** What are the strengths (& weaknesses) you bring to the task?	**RESULTS** When will you check your progress?	**CHANGES** What do you want to change?
1.				
2.				
3.				
4.				

Chapter Seven

Flexibility — The Antidote to Perfectionism

Where Did The Years Go?
by Malky Farkas Treitel

*The years
got swallowed up,
the good, the bad
and the ugly.*

*They went down
smoothly,
abruptly,
or miserably,*

*But each one
brought the gift
of understanding.*

*Each one
made me
the person
I have become.*

*Especially
the years
I would
have loved
to erase.*

"I can't put my head down peacefully on the pillow at night if something is not quite right with one of my kids — I feel a sort of unease" (*And You Thought It Was All Over,* Zenith Henkin Gross).

Do you recognize yourself in those words? Quizzes are fun because we often feel curious about encountering our inner selves. Take your own "perfectionist" pulse by giving honest answers to the questions on the following short quiz:

TRUE OR FALSE

1. Everything that goes wrong can be fixed if you have the right plan.

2. You can always take charge of your life. The answer is there. You just have to find it.

3. Everyone else is without blemish. You are the only one with a flaw.

4. People you love should be caring, respectful, and have time for you when you need them.

5. If you made a mistake, you are a mistake.

The answer to every statement above is obviously false.

However, if you evaluate how you experience each statement it may elicit a small smile. As one workshop participant so aptly commented, "Although we know these messages aren't true we feel like they are."

PERFECTION

by Gitty Kar

"When I gave birth to my first child, I thought I would be the perfect mother and she would be the perfect child. She would do anything I asked of her, and she would love me no matter what.

"Of course that did not happen. Children do their own things. My daughter was shy. No matter how nicely she sang she would not sing for the parents who came to see the school play.

"I loved dolls when I was young and I still love dolls. When my daughters were small I bought them dolls. The dolls just sat there. My older daughter loved the toy school bus and the tiny people inside, including the little doggy. My younger daughter loved Monopoly and Scrabble and not pretend play.

"Now they are grown with children of their own and they have gone on their individual paths in life. Today it is my grandchildren who are growing up. I was pleasantly surprised to learn that Brachah wants a doll with a doll carriage for her birthday. She likes dolls and plays with them for hours. My other granddaughter sang loudly in a play as I had imagined my own daughter would do.

"In the end it turned out just the way it was supposed to. I realize that my daughters were perfect for me. They will be perfect mothers for their children, although they might not realize this until their children are grown. In the meantime, I am grateful to Hashem for giving me the opportunity to enjoy my children and grandchildren."

Do you constantly aim for everything around you to be perfect? Do you wonder why things never measure up to your expectations? Do you stay up at night systematically contriving strategies to overcome your obstacles? Are you sure that if you make the right decision you can and will fix everything? Are your efforts causing emotional and physical strain?

A characteristic American approach to life is the native Yankee belief that anything that isn't working right — including kids — can be fixed if you have the right tools. Mothers can and are responsible to "fix" everything wrong and overcome every hindrance.

Mothers tend to take on more projects, more responsibilities, and more burdens than anyone else. It might be helpful to ask yourself before you start a new project, "Do I really want to do this or am I doing it because I feel I should?"

Although there is a lot we can accomplish there are also times when our efforts and intentions just don't work, no matter what. WE are limited. We might wake up early to have a calm breakfast, but the toast burns. We decide to finally settle with the I.R.S. and after an hour and a half on hold the operator cuts us off. We leave early for work and the train we are on has engine failure.

"How poor are they that have not patience! What wound did ever heal but by degrees?" (William Shakespeare, 1564-1616).

How do we feel at those times? Do these setbacks take us past the boundary of inner calm? Panic can be dangerous. On a rainy day I made a dangerous mistake while driving. I saw a red light and pressed down hard on the brake. My car skidded to the next lane. I was lucky that the street was empty. When we panic because something doesn't progress in our lives, or turn out the way we expect, we exert a lot of inner force. That force can cause a skid. If we can just calm down inside and accept the present actuality life will be easier and smoother. Is it possible to absorb day-to-day shocks with patience? One way is to realize that although we can't see a solution at the moment Hashem might be planning one for us.

Many times the things we worry about turn out better than we imagined they would. However, when we are in the middle of the crisis we panic and feel that we are without options. Remember though that just around the bend a change for the better can be waiting for us. We can learn this from an incident in *Parashas Beshalach,* where the Jews complained to Moshe when they encamped in Marah, a place that had only bitter water. The *Ibn Ezra* teaches us that the Jews stayed in Marah only one day and immediately afterward they went to Eilim — an oasis with twelve wells and seventy date palms — where they stayed for twenty days.

The Chofetz Chaim says that if the Jews had known that they would soon be leaving the place of bitter waters to camp in the lush oasis of Eilim they would have remained calm. Because we mortals have limited vision we are full of complaints when something is **presently** missing. We just have to be patient and with time most things will work out.

Rabbi Zelig Pliskin points out that when you worry you suffer in the *present* even if life turns out perfectly in the future. He advises a practical way to teach yourself to be patient instead of worrying: For one month, make a list each week of five things you worried about in the past that turned out better than you expected. You can learn from your past experience that 80 percent of the things you are worrying about *now* will be all right in the *end.* It's important to focus on the difference between the peripheral and the essential. If something will adjust with time perhaps we can handle the temporary inconvenience at present. I wrote the following essay about moving into my bungalow this past summer to help me see things from a healthier perspective.

MOVING DAY

Where is my sweater? Where are the spoons? Where are the plates? Where is the can opener? Where is the toothbrush? Is it inside or on the porch? Is it still in the car?

You may think that being on top of everything is all that matters. You try to plan carefully so that nothing will be lost. You strive for proper control. You stand guard with your permanent marker labeling boxes and bags.

Ultimately you can't swim against the current of life. Things happen. Just decide it will be O.K. You can handle it. You can still cope if things are lost for a day or two. It's not that important.

I can find comfort and calm when I realize that the people I love are where they should be. Our family is together, each one in their place. Our family is healthy and we are all under one roof. Thank you Hashem for taking care of that which is really important.

My experiences on moving day were a challenge. How will I look at the minor inconveniences caused by my mistakes? I left something behind and lost something else. I put a pot in the wrong carton. I expended a lot of effort to be perfectly in control, but inevitably some items weren't in the proper place. I had to choose — I could increase my stress level by criticizing myself over every little flaw or I could feel grateful that our family is together in one place because that is what's really important.

There is another conscious choice we can make that will put us in charge of our attitude even if we aren't in charge of our life. We can decide to smile a little more throughout the day. A musician creates a symphony with notes and we can compose our life with smiles. Learn to be comfortable and satisfied enough with the present to smile. Remember that we may be limited but we do have options. They used to say in Navardok that one should focus on wanting what one has instead of having what one wants. Laughter not only makes life pleasant, it may even be our visa to the World to Come.

LAUGHTER

Rav Beroka was walking in the market and he met Elijah the Prophet. While they spoke, two people walked into the market. Elijah indicated the two and said to Rav Beroka, "These two brothers are 'children of the World to Come.' " Rav Beroka approached them and asked, "What do you do?" They answered, "We are happy people and we cheer people up when they are sorrowful. When we see people quarreling we work hard to tell them a humorous anecdote until the two make peace with each other."

What is the meaning of the phrase "children of the World to Come"? Rabbi Akiva Eiger explains: Just as they are surely standing before you, so too, are they guaranteed the eternal rewards of the future world — without being judged and without suffering (*The World Is Built on Kindness*, p. 352).

The jesters used humor to increase peace in the community. A joke can clear the air of the poisonous fumes of a quarrel. When people are laughing they can't remain angry at each other. Perhaps you remember an instance when someone made a witty remark and saved a latently explosive situation. Wouldn't we all like to have a private jester on hand several times a day? We have within us the capacity to choose laughter instead of sadness and anger.

There were probably several hundred people in the marketplace, yet Elijah the Prophet singled out the two jesters and said that they have a guaranteed visa to the World to Come. People who spread joy are as valuable as sunshine. Sunshine is the energy that makes trees, flowers, and crops grow. Laughter is the emotional energy that helps people let go of pain and get on with life. Laughter is the sunshine that nourishes confidence, enthusiasm and optimism. Those jesters provided this precious commodity.

King Solomon said, "A glad heart cheers the face" (*Proverbs* 15:13). The secret of the vitality that can be seen shining on your face is a vibrant sense of humor. If your humor is going to be a positive factor for you it has to be healing and not hurtful to others. Surprise those around you and help them perceive and enjoy the fun in life. It's the greatest kindness.

Consider something that is irritating you now. What reaction will help the situation — anger or humor? You know the answer. Anger will just increase your pain and keep you up at night. Looking for the comical aspect will surely bring relief.

When we were babies someone could get us to laugh in five minutes. If someone played peek-a-boo, five little piggies or made a funny noise, we began giggling. You still have this ability. You just have to remember to do it. Start your personal "laughter anthology" today. Collect humorous sayings and notice the funny or silly things happening around you. Write down the sweet comments children make. It will really help you feel better while you do it and it will certainly help you feel better when you reread it in the future.

Look at the bright side in the face of gloom. Collect jokes. Call up your grandfather, he'll appreciate it so much.

Rebecca said, "My kids got into the flour at my mother-in-law's house. They looked like angels — very white and pure. The smile on their faces seemed to say, 'This is fun. This is so soft.' I got a camera and I still have the picture."

The phone rang on Thursday morning. It was Ellen. "Rosie, I just have to tell you what happened an hour ago. Remember the story Rebecca told yesterday about how her kids got into the flour and she laughed and took a picture? This morning I was not careful to fold all my kitchen chairs. I always do that before I step out of the kitchen even for a minute or my thirteen-month-old son, Zev, will climb on the counter and get into anything he finds in the cabinets. I came out of the bedroom five minutes later and he had climbed onto the kitchen table. We always have five cereal boxes out because Isaac my three-year-old can never decide which cereal to eat in the morning without tasting them all. When I came back into the kitchen, Zev was on the table sticking his hands in all five boxes and sprinkling cereal on every surface. My first impulse was to scream, but then I remembered the flour story and I began to laugh instead. My husband came in from the synagogue just then. He asked, 'What are you laughing about?' I told him the flour story and I said, 'I can't believe that less than 24 hours later our custom-made "flour" picture opportunity has arrived.' He said with a smile, 'Well, I hope you remember the flour story for the rest of your life.' "

Laughter helps you stay afloat. However, it's an emotion that may diminish as we become adults. Here are some ways to practice and evoke this positive response: Sing your children's favorite songs, exchange stories with friends, build sand castles and smash them; and make things with snow in the winter.

A smile and an encouraging word can help us communicate with our children too. It's a great way to convince children to do a chore they don't particularly enjoy. Helen said, "When I was working in camp last summer I met a parent who was unusually calm. Her children were more cooperative and helpful than average. For example, every Shabbos afternoon she would rest for an hour while an older child watched the baby. On this particular Shabbos the older sibling didn't want to babysit, although it was her turn. I've never forgotten the mother's response. Instead of shouting she smiled and said, '**I know you find this hard but if you put on a smile it will make it easier.**'

The child put the baby in the stroller and walked down the path with her. She didn't complain any more. I have told that sentence to my own children many times."

Waiting patiently for things to happen at their own pace is not a waste of time. Laughter may seem extraneous, yet actually it is essential to our well-being. The added bonus is that it helps us to uplift others. It might seem that learning a new hobby is a time waster because it takes a while to perfect the activity, but you might actually discover a wonderful hidden talent in the process.

Finally, we can regain our balance by learning to be a bit more flexible. Instead of confronting the waves of life head-on we should try to glide over them. Occasionally we have to step right in, but there are other times when we should put our life on hold — just stand aside and live this moment fully.

FLEXIBILITY

My seven-year-old sat up in bed and rubbed his eyes. He sifted through his clothes and picked up his shirt. He looked it over and said, "Thank you, Mommy, for warming it up in the dryer."

"Please, just put it on quickly," I answered.

He began buttoning his shirt. He stopped at the third button to look out the window, "Look, Mommy! I see a squirrel!" He exclaimed. "Not, now" I said. "We don't have time."

Aron never hurries. Now he is ready to put on his shoes and socks — he first examines each sock and then he pauses between the right shoe and the left one, to smile at the baby. "Aron," I exclaim. "Your bus is coming in ten minutes."

"Don't worry. I'm coming Mommy," he calls. Yet, he still has time. He has time to carefully pronounce each word of his *berachah* clearly and time to thank me, "The breakfast was so good." He catches the bus. I almost push him out the door.

I'm a master of time. I plan my morning carefully. I rush through my routine trying to complete everything on my list. I hurry and struggle to stay in control. I'm proud when I finish my list, but there are so many small pleasures I miss in the process. I'm not sure, perhaps my son understands time better than I do.

As a government leader once said, "I must govern the clock, not be governed by it."

We all want to manage our time as best we can, but if it's at the expense of enjoying life it's not such an ideal trade-off. Likewise, although we all strive to be organized and in control it's important to differentiate between major mistakes and minor mistakes. Don't amplify a minor irritation by telling yourself poisonous messages like — when will I learn how to do this, I'm so inefficient, I can't cope — when you've only made a minor mistake.

Exercise: Learning from Our Mistakes

What mistake are you worried about right now?

_____
_____
_____
_____
_____

Imagine that someone else told you about the same mistake. What would you say to help them feel better?

_____
_____
_____
_____
_____

What can you learn from this mistake? How can you benefit from what happened by taking precautions next time?

_____
_____
_____
_____
_____

Actual Responses

For the actual responses workshop participants worked in pairs. First everyone wrote the mistake that was bothering them on a little white card. After that we passed the cards around to give everyone an opportunity to write an encouraging comment. As I read the problems and responses I could see a sparkle in the women's eyes.

A door had been opened through which they saw themselves in a different light. As one participant commented, "It seems that we are a lot harder on ourselves than we are on others, perhaps we shouldn't be."

1. I was giving my in-laws a ride home when they invited my children to visit them. We were all very tired and I thought we shouldn't go, but they insisted. I agreed and in the end we went to sleep at eleven o'clock. I felt torn. It isn't good when my children go to sleep late on a school night. I wish we had gone straight home. However, I know that they would have felt hurt.

Anonymous Response: Focus on what you gave your in-laws and your children. Your children are fortunate because they can enjoy their grandparents since, thank G–d, they are healthy. Perhaps it would help if you told them in advance that the children must go to sleep early on school nights.

2. I put my son in a new yeshivah but the English program is weak. Why did I put him in this yeshivah?

Anonymous Response: Perhaps the yeshivah was good for the Hebrew curriculum. Focus your spotlight on the gain and your blindspot on the failure.

3. Yesterday my house was a total wreck. One child was in the middle of a science project in the dining room and in the kitchen we were baking for Purim. Two Rabbis walked in to leave something for my husband. I was so embarrassed.

Anonymous Response: Even with a messy house if you have a bright smiling face you can make people feel welcome. Your smile would take their attention away from the condition of the house.

4. I should write more letters. I get very lazy about writing letters to my daughter in England. Instead I just wait for her phone calls.

Anonymous Response: It doesn't have to be a long letter. Get small notepapers. Perhaps you could also send a Fax or an E-mail message.

Chapter Eight
FAITH — The Oxygen of the Soul

עֶזְרִי מֵעִם ה׳ עֹשֵׂה שָׁמַיִם וָאָרֶץ "My help is from Hashem, Maker of heaven and earth" (Tehillim 121:2).

The Brisker Rav, Rav Yitzchak Zev HaLevi Soloveitchik, achieved a very high level of trust in Hashem. Whenever the family was concerned about a material need, the Rav allayed their fears with his motto: "When you really need it, it will be there."

The Rav needed a specific medication manufactured in Switzerland. He took two pills daily. One morning his family noticed that there were only two pills left, and they had no idea when the next shipment from Switzerland was due to arrive. Someone suggested that the Rav take one pill today and save one for tomorrow, but the Rav replied, "I need two pills today; I will take both today. About tomorrow I will not worry, 'When you really need something, it will be there.' "

The next morning a total stranger knocked on the door and asked for Rabbi Soloveitchik. He explained that he had just arrived from Switzerland, where someone had approached him in the airport and asked him to deliver a small package to a certain Rabbi Soloveitchik in Israel. Inside the package were the pills.

While he was sitting *shivah,* Rav Yoshe Ber related that his departed father had once asked him, "Have you ever seen me worry even once?" (*Tehillim Treasury,* p. 143).

How do you teach someone to have *bitachon?* We are accustomed to thinking that *bitachon* is a lofty trait that is somehow beyond us. Perhaps acquiring *bitachon* needs a lot of time for contemplation and relentless soul-searching. On the contrary, it isn't like that at all. Do we have to be taught how to breathe? No, the body automatically and naturally breathes. We can take a moment to be grateful that we are all born accomplished in the art of respiration. It would be difficult indeed if one needed to learn this complex skill from others. Likewise, *bitachon* is an essential part of our being, occurring spontaneously.

In *Lev Eliyahu,* Rav Eliyahu Lopian compares *bitachon* to breathing and says, "The body naturally breathes as an automatic response. Similarly, we also have *bitachon* ingrained in us, but somehow we have stopped hearing its quiet gentle voice."

Bitachon is an integral part of us. Feeling the presence of Hashem is a natural ability with which we were all born. If we open our eyes we will observe Hashem's constant protection. We are all Hashem's children and we must merely claim our golden crown. Hashem is very close to us at all times, right in our hearts. We need only focus a particle of time, energy and attention to the inner voice of our *bitachon.*

Rav Elya Lopian explains, "A person's body needs air and food. When the air around us is fresh and pleasant scented our breathing is effortless. If, however, the air changes slightly we immediately find that we can think of nothing else. When it's cold we concentrate on catching our breath. When in a stuffy room, struggling for air makes us feel faint. We feel that if we don't get some air we'll pass out.

"A person's soul needs oxygen too. What is the soul's oxygen? Belief in Hashem! Without faith a person's soul wanes immediately. One's essence becomes brittle and dry like aging autumn leaves. A person breathes faith and without faith he cannot endure for even a short while.

"It is apparent then that man is born with the clear awareness of Hashem planted in his heart. He shouldn't have to expend effort for faith because it is the mainstay of his soul, his purpose in this world and his hope for the next. If one doesn't have to work for air and he gets it easily and continuously, surely he is provided with the oxygen of the soul" (*Lev Eliyahu*, part 1).

SHARING EXPERIENCES

I asked the women who attend my weekly workshops — "When did you feel cheerful in the last week? When did you feel that Hashem was right there helping and guiding you?"

Together with the women who attend the weekly *shiur* we gathered good feelings. We thought of an eighteen-month-old proudly screaming, *Amen!* or a surprise cup of coffee brought to you by your big third grader. We mentioned baking *challah*, shopping for Shabbos and writing down the recipe for our first *chulent*. We all liked new *sefarim*.

Someone mentioned that *mitzvos* awaken our feelings of *bitachon*. Someone else said, "I feel that Hashem knows when I need encouragement. It's happened a few times that when I felt lonely, I found a letter in the mailbox or the phone rang and it was a '*Nachas* call.' "

There is the inspiration of Yom Kippur, the delicate smell of the *esrog*. There is the joy of receiving letters in the mailbox from Israel. There is the comfort of waking up late on Shabbos morning, and the intrigue of a bird's nest outside your window. There is your friend calling to talk when you felt lonely.

There are surprise guests just when the house looks great. There is the second *Seder* — when you have had a chance to rest. A doctor smiling at you and saying, "The results are back. All the tests were negative! It's definitely not that frightening thing you were afraid to mention by name."

There is the memory of one's first *siddur*. Sunset at the *Kosel*. Holding a newborn. Meeting someone you admire. Flowers. Putting up the Shabbos *blech* and this week you are early! Leaves changing color in the fall. When everyone likes everything you made for Shabbos. There is the special smell of *be-samim* at *Havdalah*. There are alumni classes and reunions. There are hundreds of men rushing to *shul* with their sons on Friday night. There is coming home and everyone running to the door joyously calling — Mommy!

Clearly we could have gone on and on. We sat together until 12:40 although the lecture ends at 12:00. People were dancing out, singing compliments behind them like, "This was such fun. Thank you. I know I want to come back. Your lecture made my day."

EMBELLISH THE GOOD

I realize that the best way to feel close to Hashem is to pause and savor the lovely occurrences that happen every day. It is up to us to put them on the map and turn them into milestones. As Goldie said, "If you want to feel uplifted it's not enough to notice the good in passing. You have to embellish the good." Embellish is defined as, "to endow with beauty and elegance by way of a notable addition."

Awareness of Hashem is all around you. Use your G-d given senses and trust that you will see Hashem's wisdom around you when you allow yourself the opportunity. Discover the splendor of each moment. You really can feel Hashem's presence around you and in you.

What is beauty? What is indisputably valuable and beautiful and what is just pretty superficially? Is there a prototype of beauty that everyone pursues that is only superficial? Is there a true beauty that we take for granted? When Chaya described a childhood memory in one of her lectures I began asking myself these questions.

"I grew up in Jerusalem. We were poor. Life was a daily struggle to survive. We used to get packages from America. Once my mother got a lovely black velour robe that had ten sequin buttons marching down the front. I was about five and every Shabbos I'd admire my mother's robe.

"I would look at the robe and pretend that the lovely buttons were real diamonds. 'Tomorrow, we will go to the store and they will tell us that the buttons are real diamonds. We will be able to get many things we need. We can get new chairs, a soft sofa, new shoes. Perhaps mother will buy me a doll.' I played this imaginary game quite often. Each time I'd imagine a different list of items we could buy if only the buttons were real diamonds.

"Of course, although the robe was pretty the sparkling buttons were just sequins. Many years later my first grandchild was born. It was so thrilling to actually attend my grandson's *bris*. There are many thoughts that swirl through our minds at a time like that. I didn't expect that my mother's black velour Shabbos robe would be one of them.

"Am I not enjoying life's greatest beauty without stopping to look and savor it? Do I go about my daily life thinking of my many blessings as sequins when truly I have diamonds all around me?

"I pondered. Our life was difficult in many ways but wasn't it beautiful? Wasn't it more precious and valuable than anything the diamonds could have bought? We have a large family that is truly devoted to following the Torah path. Now my father can be at his great grandson's *bris* and the chain of tradition continues. I turned to my mother and said, "*Ima,* remember the sequins on the robe? Well, you really had diamonds and they are right here in this room."

Bitachon develops in you when you think about it. With a bit of effort you can find many opportunities to sing to Hashem every day. Rabbi Eliezer Papo in the *sefer Pele Yo'aitz* describes the benefits of faith. *"When you look at life with open eyes you perceive how Hashem is supporting and guiding each person. This will develop your enthusiasm for mitzvos and you will take greater precautions to remain pure from sin. You will gain a lion's boldness for Hashem's service. Nothing will stop you because you will feel in your heart that Hashem is with you. Hashem sees, Hashem hears and the good you do is recorded and remembered. You will have complete faith that the righteous await a good reward and the wicked a severe punishment. You will understand that when it is difficult to perform a good deed its reward is greater ... "*

Imagine:

What would you achieve if you felt supported in your endeavors? How would it feel to welcome each day with enthusiasm and courage? How would persisting despite difficulty transform your life?

These are the benefits the *Pele Yo'aitz* has guaranteed to those who master *bitachon*. You can feel secure and protected, loved and nurtured. Experience awareness of Hashem. It's all around you!

There are two ways one affects the world. You can influence others by actively speaking with them and motivating them to follow your banner. Perhaps an article you write will be published, or a newspaper will interview you and include your picture. Torah consciousness maintains that we also affect the world by our actions, even when they are behind closed doors, in the privacy of our homes. How does peace in one's home affect the world?

"Whenever there is peace in a house, it is as if there is peace in the entire world" (*Avos d'Rabi Nosson*). The home is where everything originates.

Every Jewish home represents the Tabernacle. If the man and wife are worthy, the *Shechinah*, the Divine Presence, is there just as it was in the Tabernacle (*Sotah* 17a).

How many *mitzvos* which we are able to do just slip through our fingers? Maybe it was a *Minchah* that we put off saying until it was too late. Perhaps it's a phone call to a lonely person. We can all think of numerous examples. These missed opportunities fill us with regret. The antidote is determination. With an ounce of determination a lot of good can be accomplished. Many times I've sighed and said aloud, "I feel so guilty." My husband turns and says with a smile, "Don't feel guilty. Do something!"

Chapter Nine
Gratitude — My Little Book of Magic

You are ready! You definitely yearn to improve your life. Hold on tightly to those feelings!

On a scale of 1-10, how vital is it to you to have a good day, a good week, a good life?

Write your number on the line:_____

Don't stop now to think about how you've tried to improve in the past and yet are still anchored in the same spot. That line of thinking is an obstacle to the changes you want to make. Just direct your focus to your goal. You *need* and *want* to have a better life.

You are standing on the threshold of a revolutionary experience. There is a practical tool you can use that will free you to enjoy life more completely. It will help you focus on the unique person Hashem designed you to be.

When you drive from New York to Montreal there are two things which must be clear even before you look at the map to plan your route. First, you have to know where Montreal is located. Second, you must also determine your starting point. Only then can you find the correct route on the map to your destination. At this point, it is also necessary for you to think about precisely where you are and where you want to be.

HOW TO USE THE INVENTORY CHART

Rate how you are currently feeling in general about each area of your life by selecting from the following scale of feelings — numbered 1 to 6 — the one which describes your feelings best.

Scale of Feelings:
1- Unhappy, hollow 2- Fairly disappointed 3- Mixed feelings
4- Fairly pleased 5- Very delighted 6- Absolutely joyous

INVENTORY				
	WEEK 1	WEEK 2	WEEK 3	WEEK 4
MAIN VENTURE				
RELATIONSHIPS				
FAMILY				
FRIENDS				
PERSONAL GROWTH				
BELIEFS				
TORAH KNOWLEDGE				
PRAYER				
EMOTIONS				
TIME				
GOALS				
INTERESTS				
HUMOR				
GENERAL HEALTH				
SUCCESS				
OTHER				

USING THE CHART IN THE FUTURE

Follow the instructions as you did originally. If you incorporate the techniques in this chapter and in the other sections of the book you should see your attitude improve on subsequent occasions. Measuring your improvement can be very encouraging.

The technique that follows is simultaneously simple and difficult. It's an easy way to gain insight and penetrate your essence. It's difficult because it will only work if you are determined to persevere. It won't work if you just read about it, or only try it halfheartedly. Please decide to ponder the following idea carefully. It holds a significant key to acquiring A CALM HEART that has worked in hundreds of lives.

We can change our reality by creating pictures in our mind.

As Rabbi Bachya Ibn Pekudah said in the *Chovos HaLevavos,* "Whenever your mind is free, make a conscious effort to focus on the good that the A–mighty has bestowed upon you."

In everyday life, pay attention to the compliments you receive in your daily encounters, recognize your progress in your work, and count your small triumphs. Decide that you will have a healthy and vital attitude. Noticing the good in your life is the first step, but there is also a practical way to cherish life's blessings.

The blessings of our life tend to blend with the humdrum of our daily routine. However, if we have a special place to save and savor Hashem's generous gifts, their benefits are enhanced.

You need a place to record and take stock of your grateful thoughts. A notebook, for example, is useful for collecting your triumphs and constructing your dreams. It can be your tangible site to generate magic. In your journal you may record the blessings of your life and your enthusiastic feelings. Look for positive circumstances and gifts of largesse and write them down. True, there are trials and tribulations, but you still can find many positive things to be glad about in your situation. This will help bolster your spirits. It will also make you aware of all the positive things with which Hashem has blessed you and yours. I call this book a *"Baruch Hashem* Book."

I have kept a *Baruch Hashem* Book for five years and I feel that it helps me face the daily challenges of life. I have always been sure that our Torah sages know the value of gratitude, but I somehow couldn't find a specific Torah thought related to appreciating Hashem's daily goodness. Now that I yearn to share this concept with all of you, Hashem helped me find a source for it.

I was glancing through the *sefer Ohr Yechezkel* when I read the following magnificent Torah thought.

"I was aroused and inspired when I learned the verse in *Parashas Bereishis,* כִּי לֹא הִמְטִיר ה' אֱלֹקִים עַל הָאָרֶץ וְאָדָם אַיִן ... (2:5). *Rashi* explains that Hashem did not cause the rain to fall until He created man because before then there was nothing that could recognize the value of rain.

"We learn from this that the way of Heaven is for bounty to descend only when there is someone to experience it and proclaim gratitude to Hashem. If we see an abundance of Hashem's generosity in the world it is only in the merit of the rare *tzaddik* who is worthy of it because of his gratitude to Hashem. The others enjoy Hashem's bounty in the merit of the *tzaddik.* Furthermore, when people enjoys Hashem's good without recognizing its Heavenly source they are actually borrowing and will have to repay at a steep price. As we are told in *Avos,* 'Every pleasure in this world is granted as a loan.' On this Rabbi Yisrael Salanter commented, 'This world is an extravagant hotel.'

"From all this we can appreciate how much one gains through a profound examination of Hashem's kindness ... when he says a *berachah.* This is the best means to strengthen one's *bitachon*" (*Ohr Yechezkel,* p. 178).

Rav Yechezkel Levenstein teaches us here that we earn the privilege of enjoying Hashem's bounty by demonstrating our gratitude to Him. He points out that gratitude causes Hashem blessing to reach the world and that gratitude pays for the pleasures we consume. If we don't say our blessings now there will be a steep price to pay later. A *Baruch Hashem* Book makes our life better by channeling Hashem's blessings to us. It can also help us cultivate optimism and courage.

Life's vicissitudes can be frightening and discouraging for our children. Our children hear about tragedies every day. My fourteen-year-old daughter came to me and asked, "Mommy why are so many bad things happening?" I suggested that she begin a *Baruch Hashem* Book and notice that many good things are happening too. Chavah started her *Baruch Hashem* Book in April. Now she has almost 2,000 items on her *Baruch Hashem* list. She even took the book along to sleep-away camp. Many workshop participants and friends have started their books and say they are smiling more frequently. It helps children, mothers and grandmothers. It's easy to begin.

This one little book has made all the difference in the world for me. It helps me handle fear and worry. I realize that although there are problems there are good things happening too. It helps me be aware that Hashem is always at my side. I can look back and count the ways Hashem has led me and helped me.

I can also count the ways that Hashem has helped others. I write down births, engagements, the successes of people I know, as well as my own triumphs. Three weeks ago a friend, a Shabbos guest, got engaged. She wanted so much to start a family. She is 38 years old. *Baruch Hashem.*

I count the *Shabbosos* that everyone was healthy. The *Shabbosos* that I didn't have to worry as I touched a feverish head. I smile because I feel wealthy. *Baruch Hashem.*

Somehow children are so easily fascinated with life. A trip to the park and an ice-cream cone has all the significance of a trip to Paris for them. As we get older our days just run into each other and it's easy to feel that we are running in circles. This magic little book helps you focus on the many treasures you'd never notice otherwise.

Do you sometimes tell yourself, "I never do anything special"? In this little magic book you can record the small ways you help others. It can encourage you to dream of more ambitious ways you can give of yourself and become a better person.

It's not difficult to start writing your own *Baruch Hashem* Book. You can start simple; a spiral notebook and a 25-cent pen is adequate. You don't need special talent. It only takes a few minutes a day. You may record things privately or find someone to share it with. And you will get so much. You will find your dreams, your hopes, your happiness.

Your magic book accomplishes several things at one time. It can make your faith in Hashem grow. It can help you see the good in your life. It will energize you and cure your boredom. It can also generate hope.

On top of each page I write "Thank You Hashem." Then I simply list the good things that happened that day. I started five years ago and my *Baruch Hashem* list has grown to an incredible 17,150 entries!! So now I have 17,150 things to be happy about and it helps me maintain a cheerful disposition. At first I used an unadorned notebook, but once I realized that I'd really want to save these books I began using fabric-covered blank books for my lists.

Perhaps one of the earliest *Baruch Hashem* lists recorded is in the *sefer Chovos HaLevavos,* by Rabbi Bachya Ibn Pekudah. In the chapter *Cheshbon HaNefesh* (which is about 20 pages long) he calls on everyone to make a penetrating inner accounting of the basic advantages we all share. Perhaps you'd like to begin your *Baruch Hashem* list with these concepts. I listed the first three points here to give you a sample to taste. You can explore *Chovos HaLevavos* for an in- depth analysis.

> "Think about Hashem's kindness at your birth. You were nothing and you became something. You hadn't yet earned the right to exist. Hashem in His generosity brought you into the world. He positioned you in a good spot. You are on a higher level than rocks, plants and

animals. If you think about this you will comprehend that you should thank Hashem for this.

"Second, thank Hashem for His kindness in creating you complete with healthy organs and limbs. Hashem has kept you basically healthy since birth. Imagine — if you were born without eyes, ears or hands and a doctor would restore those limbs to you. Wouldn't you honor that doctor and feel indebted to him? How much greater is Hashem's kindness in creating you with perfect wisdom right from the start. King David praised Hashem in this way when he said, רַבּוֹת עָשִׂיתָ אַתָּה ה' אֱלֹקַי נִפְלְאֹתֶיךָ וּמַחְשְׁבֹתֶיךָ אֵלֵינוּ — *Much have you done, You Hashem, my God, Your wonders and Your thoughts are for us* (*Tehillim* 40:6).

"Third, thank Hashem for the ability to learn, understand and speak. Your wisdom far surpasses the animals and birds. Our lives do not suffice to thank and praise our Creator for the endless kindness of wisdom."

I listed about three hundred basic advantages in the beginning of my book. Then I began noting the average good things that happen every day. Here are some of the things I've listed recently in my *Baruch Hashem* Book.

QUARTERS FOR THE METER

I was shopping at my sister's new store. My niece looked out the window and noticed the meter maid approaching. She quickly took six quarters out of the cash register and ran outside. Then she deposited a quarter in each meter on the block. The meter maid was indignant, "Do you mean to tell me that these are all your father's cars?" With a radiant smile my niece said, "That's my father's car and that one is my uncle's; that one is my cousin's car and that one is my sister's. We're all one family!"

MAZEL TOV!

Baruch Hashem it's been a month of miracles. A beautiful baby girl was born on the third of Elul at 1:45. Her name is

Sheva Rochel. She keeps me busy 24 hours a day. Sheva Rochel was born on the birthday of my oldest daughter Chavah who is fourteen.

Everyone is busy wondering what color her eyes will be. Will her hair become blond? Who does she look like? Does she look intelligent? Is she smiling or is it our imagination?

MAKE A GREAT DAY

In the beginning of this chapter I asked, "Do you want to have a great day?" Basy, my telephone *chavrusah*, shared an important lesson with me that she learned from her friend.

"I no longer tell people to HAVE a great day, instead I tell them, 'MAKE a great day.' When I wake up in the morning I remind myself — today is in my control. Even if the kids are at home because they are under the weather, I can have a great day. It depends on how I look at everything moment by moment, hour by hour, and that's up to me. When my husband comes home at night and asks, 'How was your day?' I answer, 'It was good!' "

The "*Baruch Hashem* Book" will help you discover Hashem's gifts, today, tomorrow and twenty years from now. It will help you **make a great day!**

LIFE-CHANGING BENEFITS OF THE "*BARUCH HASHEM* BOOK"

BENEFIT ONE: You will learn more about your talents and the unique person you are. You will feel motivated to accomplish more every day.

BENEFIT TWO: You will begin to notice that you have many things to be happy about. You'll have easy access to successes and triumphs that would otherwise be overlooked.

BENEFIT THREE: Everything we enjoy in the world needs a *berachah*. We must acknowledge Hashem and thank Him for everything He gives us. When we bless Hashem and thank Him,

Hashem grants us more bounty and reward. *Kol hamevarech misbarech* (*Pele Yo'aitz — Berachah*).

BENEFIT FOUR: Gratitude to Hashem activates our enthusiasm. We feel motivated to serve Hashem completely with love and with great joy (*Pele Yo'aitz — Berachah*).

Chapter Ten

Smart Habits for Stressful Times

1. HABIT: MAKING BETTER CHOICES

ACTION: List three things you really want to do. Decide how you will accomplish them. Choose a reasonable deadline. (Don't become too ambitious. It's better to limit yourself to three goals and actually achieve them.)

BENEFIT: Success in one area leads to success in many other areas. Following through on decisions is a skill. By setting attainable goals and achieving them you train yourself to think reasonably and work steadily until you accomplish your goal. The advantages of this are obvious and need no further emphasis.

2. HABIT: MAKING DECISIONS

ACTION: Ask yourself, "When has my decision led to good results?"

BENEFIT: The awareness that you have successfully made responsible choices in the past can help you make good choices now. Sometimes we are not able to achieve what we want. Instead of feeling discouraged we should remember decisions in the past that worked well. This will help us to use *all* our present opportunities well. Don't miss out on every opportunity because of one disappointment.

3. HABIT: TAKE THE INITIATIVE

ACTION: Instead of waiting for someone else to act, you should take the initiative.

Brenda said, "I decided it would be nice to go to a *Rosh Chodesh* brunch. It was the day before *Rosh Chodesh* and no one had called to invite me. I realized that I'd have to make the party myself. I invited some friends to a *Rosh Chodesh* brunch at my house. It was a beautiful party and one of the guests offered to make a brunch next month at her house."

BENEFIT: If you take the initiative there are many ways you can improve many people's lives, including your own. Instead of being enveloped in self-pity take control and do something!

4. HABIT: STAY CALM

ACTION: If something breaks and it can be fixed or replaced accept the mishap calmly.

BENEFIT: When we remain calm our family enjoys peace and Hashem's presence dwells in our home. "Whenever there is peace in the house it is as if there is peace in the entire world" (*Avos d'Rabi Nosson*).

5. HABIT: LAUGHTER

ACTION: Collect humorous anecdotes each week to which you can refer in order to relieve tension.

BENEFIT: Laughter not only makes life pleasant, it may even be your visa to the World to Come (see p. 76).

6. HABIT: SMILE

ACTION: Give a smile and some pleasant words to your family, friends and neighbors.

BENEFIT: "A glad heart cheers the face" (*Proverbs* 15:13).

7. HABIT: GRATITUDE

ACTION: On a piece of paper write *Baruch Hashem*. Then list the good things that happened today.

BENEFIT: "When we bless Hashem and thank Him, Hashem grants us additional bounty and reward" (*Pele Yo'aitz*).

8. HABIT: FAITH

ACTION: Make a list of all your worries and pack them away with the Pesach dishes. Faith is like oxygen for the soul.

BENEFIT: When you take out the list next year you will see that Hashem has helped you with your worries. This will be a tangible reminder to strengthen your *bitachon*. What may strengthen the awakening of faith is looking into all the good things that Hashem, Blessed be He, does with a man at all periods and times, and into the great wonders that He does with him from the time of his birth until his last day (*Mesillas Yesharim*, Ch. 8).

9. HABIT: FLEXIBILITY

ACTION: Recognize that there is more than one approach to a situation.

BENEFIT: Flexibility allows for options and reduces disappointments and frustrations.

Words
Habits
Actions
Thoughts

Chapter Eleven

Serenity Through Simplicity

GIVING

by Malky Farkas Treitel

The best way
to feel good
is to go out
and help others.

The surest way
of getting
is by giving.

If you want
to change,
assume that
you have.

If you
believe it,
then you
are there.

Every night the skies gradually become dark, and there is an awesome sunset of orange, red, yellow, and purple light. Do we ever stop to think why the sunset is so exquisite? I think that the sunset is designed to teach us that our day was meant to end with beauty. Since I live in the city, I can glimpse only three inches of this beauty between the buildings and skyscrapers. Occasionally, when I take a moment to look at my mini-sunset here in New York it reminds me of a huge sunset I once experienced near the Dead Sea in Israel. Recalling the comfort and pure friendship that I felt under the purple sky is uplifting.

We were a group of 80 students. There was just our group and the desert as God created it. There was nothing man-made, nothing polluted to obstruct our view or to distract our minds. There among the sand, rocks and caves the awesome beauty spoke to us. One quickly runs out of words and exclamations to describe one's feelings at such a time. We saw a new world that we had never before seen, and the beauty took our breath away.

There was a feeling of closeness and unity amongst us. We sat in concentric circles with arms clasped and sang slow songs. Some girls took out their guitars and played soft chords to accompany the singing. Our music echoed for miles into the silence that surrounded us. One felt a longing to remember this exquisite evening forever, a longing that was like a bubble soaring inside us. We were a circle of equals under God's beauty.

Take a moment now to relax and imagine a peaceful scene. Try to capture the relaxed calm feeling of a mind at rest. Concentrate on each breath. Try to imagine your chest rising and falling in a slow, steady rhythm. With each breath, feel a warm comforting glow that is just right. As you breathe out, let go of the tension and intense emotions.

Relaxation is a deep pleasure, and yet it costs nothing. Every person, rich and poor alike, has a common need to nurture his inner self, to nourish his heart and mind. If you want, at some point, to have a calm heart, every day see yourself as the calm person you want to be.

When I share my sunset story with my workshop group, I usually notice at least two or three people smiling. They try to hold it in, but they look as though they are about to burst out laughing. "What's so funny?" I ask.

"Well, perhaps we are supposed to find peace in whatever our day brings, but that's just not how it is in reality. Who has time to look at the sunset? Often I feel uncomfortable rather than calm and peaceful; I'm tired and irritable. I'm plagued by my worries. My back acts up and my sore tooth throbs."

When these comments come up I tell my listeners that it is normal to think that our challenges control us. The advantage of that line of reasoning is that it absolves us of responsibility for our attitude. However, as a result we lose out, because if our thoughts just happen and we are helpless victims, there is no way for us to break the cycle. The truth is that stress is a result of a series of improper choices we have made on all levels — physical, emotional, and spiritual, as the folk tale below illustrates. The benefit of acknowledging our responsibility for our stress is that it empowers us to improve our situation.

In the days of the horse-drawn conveyance, a traveler arrived at a train station and hired a cab. After giving the driver his destination, he cautioned him, "Please avoid this particular road. There is a deep ditch there."

The driver replied, "Just sit back and relax, my friend. Don't worry. I have been driving these roads for 35 years."

As they proceeded the passenger said, "I can see the way you are heading. Please don't go that way. The road there has that big pit."

The driver smiled reassuringly. "No need to fear," he said. "I have been driving these roads for 35 years."

Soon they turned off onto a path. The passenger shouted, "Hey! This is the path I told you to avoid. It has this great big ditch ahead."

"Stop worrying," the driver said. "Haven't I told you? I have been driving these roads for 35 years."

Before long, they reached the ditch and fell in, wagon, horse, driver and passenger. The driver crawled out from beneath the wreckage.

"Funny thing, I swear," he said. "I have been driving these roads for 35 years, and every time I pass here, this is what always happens!" (*Generation to Generation,* Rabbi Abraham J. Twerski M.D.).

How aptly this story describes our human tendencies! We follow the same route day after day, unwilling to admit that we have relinquished control over our behavior; and — just like the driver in the story — we realize it when it's too late. Take, for instance, the classic syndrome of the mid-afternoon slump. Day after day, we sit back and wait for the familiar sluggish feeling to come over us. But it doesn't have to be that way.

I'm sure you are aware that children don't have to work hard to relax. They can fall asleep on the floor in the middle of a game or just put their head down on the kitchen table and drift off. We probably never noticed when our difficulty with stress began because it happened so gradually. A child's life is much simpler than ours. They don't worry about finances, health, taxes, or the state of the world. They don't have a ton of information weighing down their mind. Is all the information with which we are bombarded good for us? Perhaps our modern, fast-paced existence isn't letting us find the peace of mind we crave. We tend to visualize a barrier as a brick wall, but other things will do just as well in separating us from ourselves. If the music plays too loudly, it's impossible to hear yourself think.

When the stress in my life mounts and seems like a solid impenetrable wall I remember Tifrach. Tifrach is a town in the south of Israel that is so small that we had trouble finding it when we visited there during spring vacation in our school days. It was so quiet there that I heard the birds singing, the bees buzzing, and the wind blowing through the leaves. The residents of Tifrach have much less than I do, but they aren't worried about it because they need much less.

We rode on the bus for an hour and a half, heading south from Jerusalem. The bus stopped and we got off. We saw nothing but fields and heard only the wind whispering in the tall grass. "Where is Tifrach?" I asked my friend Sharon. "Can you see any houses or streets?"

Sharon shrugged. "The only things at this bus stop are a bus stop sign, two paved roads leading away from the junction, and tall grass. This is the right stop. Did you get any directions?"

"The teacher who sent us here simply said to get off at the stop and walk ten minutes and 'you can't miss it,'" I replied as I peered into the distance.

Where was this hamlet? No one had told us that there were two roads. We started walking down the road. We walked and looked and searched. We hoped to hear the usual noises of civilization, but all we heard was a deep stillness. Occasionally several birds chirped in lively conversation and when we passed a patch of red wildflowers a few bees buzzed around. After about half an hour we saw a clearing in the distance. We walked another quarter mile and knocked on the door of the first house. "Is this Tifrach?" we asked.

"Tifrach is down the other road," the girl told us.

"Does that mean that we have to walk all the way back?" we asked in panic.

"Don't worry — there's a shortcut. You see the mud path? Just go straight. You can see the houses from here."

We peered into the distance; **we** couldn't see any houses.

"It's easy; you'll be able to find it," she reassured us.

We nodded but our eyes were confused.

"I'll tell you what," she said. "Just to make you feel better, I'll walk you there."

After another 20 minutes of walking through tall grass we suddenly saw the low homes of Tifrach before us. "Thank you — thank you so much," we said.

"Don't worry, it was nothing — and Shabbat Shalom." Our guide waved as she ran back down the road.

This was Tifrach: two large buildings parallel to each other and two circles of houses. It looked like a large figure eight. Where was everyone? A girl, not more than four-years-old, ran up to us, "You are coming to us. Let me show you the way. You are late."

I glanced at my watch. "We arrived at the junction an hour and a half ago, but we got lost. It took us just as long to get here from the bus stop as it did for us to travel from Jerusalem."

"How can you get lost ?" exclaimed the four-year-old. "It's so easy. I'm Sari Obermeister. You are going to have my room." She walked us to the door and ran off.

The house was spacious, but everything was simple. The furnishings were functional and not for show. Mrs. Obermeister greeted us with a calm smile. Her dress was of faded flowered fabric and she wore an apron. We were conscious of how fancy our own dresses were by comparison, although when we had left Jerusalem our clothes had seemed to be average everyday clothes.

I still remember the cake and coffee that Mrs. Obermeister served us. It was vanilla cake with a thick chocolate icing. My mouth waters now as I think about it; I should have asked for that recipe. I marveled, while I ate, at the serenity of this place. It was only an hour and a half away from busy Jerusalem and yet we were in a wonderfully different world. It was my first encounter with life in a town garnished with trees and fields, comfortable uncluttered homes, and lots of open space. There was no honking of car horns, no stores with glitzy windows, no traffic lights, no pavement. Life here was so noiseless and uncomplicated!

Four-year-old Sari took us on a tour of Tifrach. She showed us peach trees covered with green peaches, caterpillars and cocoons, the vegetable garden and several birds' nests. Each thing she pointed out caused us to exclaim in wonder. Finally Sari said, "What's the matter ? Haven't you seen any of this before?" Should we have admitted that we hadn't?

A soft stillness surrounded us. It wasn't just that there was no noise; it was quieter than that. You could actually hear the birds singing. I felt so calm and happy.

When we came back, I overheard my hostess talking with one of her older daughters.

"Can I wear the dress we were saving for Pesach this week?" the girl asked.

"Why?"

"I forgot to wash my other nice dress."

"Don't worry," the mother assured her. "I washed and ironed it for you. It's hanging near the porch."

I was amazed. Did this girl have only two nice dresses? Was her only worry about her dress that it should be clean? Everyone around me was so secure and content. I wondered if it were possible that a simple lifestyle could give you that.

Whenever I start to get tense, I make a list of the many things I have to do and think for a moment that almost everything on my list has to do with things they don't even have in Tifrach — and yet they live quite nicely there. I remember the uncomplicated life I saw there and ask myself, "Is it really that urgent?" The world I saw in Tifrach puts the trivia in my life in proper perspective.

What are the gifts of a simple life-style? Can we distill the simple environment in which peace of mind thrives into several key elements that can be transplanted into our lives? I feel that wherever we are, there are always elements of the Tifrach experience that we can use. Once we identify what's needed to make our lives more serene we can begin incorporating those factors into our lives.

I remember the serenity on everyone's face in that tiny town, an inner tranquility that came from having a clear purpose in life. The children were free to live every moment fully and they exhibited an independence and confidence that grows in an atmosphere where competition is minimal. The children came and went freely and managed so much on their own. The neighbors were friendly and ready to help one another. They were united by a common goal. I'm convinced that a slow pace of life leads to a steady and healthy outlook.

SIMPLICITY!

Here is a practical four-step plan to take charge of your life.

1. Take action.

When I observed and admired the many beautiful gardens that young children had planted and tended in Tifrach, I learned that activity is the key to satisfaction. When the stress is too much for you, don't sit back and analyze. Do something constructive. When you take action, it helps you relax.

2. A small success brings a larger success.

Four-year-old Sari had more skills and more confidence than any child of her age that I have ever met. This may be because she had more opportunities to try new things and to succeed than other children her age. Tackle one "bite-size" part of an overwhelming task that confronts you. The success will give you peace of mind.

3. Don't drown in paper.

There seemed to be more room in the Obermeister's small home in Tifrach than there is in my larger one. Everything was organized and tidy. Could it be because they don't have to arrange the jumble of extraneous items/materials that I am bombarded with?

While there is a lot of reading material that helps us grow intellectually, the reading we engage in to relax might not help us feel calm. Mail, newspapers, magazines, and catalogs eat up our time and may make us feel flustered.

Sometimes sitting quietly in a peaceful spot outside can be a better break than skimming through a catalog. Where is your inner voice? Who are you? How can you know if you don't take a break from the flood of information?

4. Silence is golden.

There was so much that I could hear in the quiet atmosphere of that farm in the south of Israel that I have never been able to hear elsewhere. They are sounds that exist only in the silence. Once you experience that peaceful voice you always long to hear it again. Nighttime is a good time for listening. Listen to your child's breathing. Listen to a bird outside. Listen to yourself think. All of these are sounds that can only be appreciated in silence.

One of the early sages taught, "I have found nothing better for oneself than silence" (*Avos* 1:17). A person will not tire of being quiet. We should not only stop speaking from time to time, but also take a break from physical pursuits and concentrate on the spiritual, to give our body the quiet time it needs.

Rav Simchah Zissel, the dean of the Yeshivah in Kelm, Lithuania was an authority on peace of mind. He suggested to his students two exercises to help strengthen this ability. When you wish to tell someone a piece of news, wait at least 15 minutes before you relate it. When someone asks you for advice, don't give an immediate reply. Think over your response for at least five minutes.

This advice is not as easy as it sounds. I tried to cut the time I waited before speaking by about a third. I waited five minutes before picking up the phone when I had the impulse to relate a piece of news, and two minutes before answering a question. Waiting even two minutes was a difficult habit to learn, yet it did slow down the pace of my racing mind. It also helped me to stop putting my foot in my mouth so often. I'm trying to gradually build up my quiet time to the recommended amount.

QUIET TIME
by Cipora Shazuri Weber

I have to go to Monsey today. I'm looking forward to some quiet time. I might even have a seat to myself. I can close my eyes and relax or enjoy the beautiful scenery as the bus travels to its destination.

Oh no! I think I am in trouble. I see the town *yenta* waiting on line to board the bus. I'll close my eyes. Perhaps she won't notice me. The thought of her myriad questions make me cringe.

"Hi, how are you? How many children do you have? Are they all married? Do you mind if I sit next to you?" She doesn't wait for my answer. She sits down and continues her questions. "How many grandchildren? Who did they marry? What do they do for a living? Are your sons and sons-in-law learning?" I wonder, is she really listening to the answers? She fires questions so quickly.

"I remember hearing that your daughter is a principal and your other daughter writes novels. What does your poor son do? By the way do you know So-and-so? I wonder if there is something wrong. She's so quiet all the time. Do you think she has something to hide? By the way, why are you going to Monsey today?"

"Excuse me," my seat mate said. "I see my neighbor coming. I had better go and sit next to her. I'll talk to you soon."

I breathe deeply and sigh. What a relief! I hope no one will notice the now empty seat at my side. Is there a way I can hide? Doesn't anyone want to have some solitude? Can they just sit next to you without talking? If I plug in my Walkman, perhaps I won't be interrupted. Hashem, please. Can I have time to think by myself?

Someone has recognized me and is approaching my seat. I shrink into the seat and cringe inside. "Oh excuse me, I didn't see you. How are you feeling? Is everything all right? Why are you hunched over? Can I sit here?" She doesn't wait for an answer and sits down anyway.

The conversation begins. "I finally got that raise I asked for. Do you remember the woman I told you was pregnant? She had triplets. Isn't it great?" My curiosity was aroused. Just as she was becoming really interesting she said, "We better stop chatting. Some people never know when to keep quiet. Everyone needs a chance to relax on a bus ride now and then." Before I could ask another question, my neighbor closed her eyes, nodded her head and fell asleep. Her breathing was rhythmic and steady. She sounded like she had been sleeping for many hours in a row.

Do you know how five minutes of silence feels? When was the last time you tried to stop everything and think peacefully?

Exercise: How Long Is a Minute?

Right now take five minutes and just listen to yourself think. Pause and write down your thoughts below as they enter in your mind. Don't edit; just write what comes.

_____

_____

_____

_____

_____

_____

Actual Responses

1. I was thinking about how many times I've done something I later regretted because I didn't take the necessary time to think first.

2. It was very comforting to take time out to think. I paused to remember that G-d watches over us and takes care of us.

3. I am not feeling well today. During this minute I had the chance to tell myself, "G-d took care of me under worse conditions and I completely rely on Him now."

4. Instead of letting my life get so hectic because I tend to depend on myself for everything, I should ask for a little help.

5. Nothing on this earth is what it seems. We tend to live superficially; we get caught up in the mundane and we just exist. The deeper meaning is there and when we pause for a minute, we remember life's significance.

6. I was thinking about how often we panic for no reason. Yesterday I was locked out of my house. I had left an elaborate cake baking in the oven. I tried my neighbor who had a spare set of my keys but she wasn't home. I thought I was getting heart palpitations. My friend came home from shopping five minutes later and my cake was fine.

PRACTICAL TIPS

SAVE YOUR FAVORITE PICTURES

Beautiful things are soothing. Pictures of the awe-inspiring outdoors, such as the view from a mountain or a magnificent sunset revive and comfort the spirit. If you actually visited the area, pictures are twice as meaningful because they help you remember and relive your relaxing experience.

DISCONNECT YOUR PHONE FOR AN HOUR

Plan to give yourself some solitude and a chance to slow down. Talking prevents you from relaxing. Phone conversations often leave us worked up or excited.

SOURCES OF HARMONY

Sources of harmony counterbalance the stress in our lives. Set up routines in your schedule to give yourself a treat each evening: a hot bath, an enjoyable music tape, a vase of fresh flowers, a book that is encouraging and hopeful.

SIMPLE TASKS

Plan to perform simple tasks that you can finish and that will give you a feeling of accomplishment and satisfaction.

SERENE MEMORIES

Walking home under a black sky, I look up at the heavens and the sparkling stars. Tonight I feel closer to those stars than on any other night of the year. The street is quiet. There are hundreds of Jews walking home around me, yet everyone is quiet. Occasionally you hear someone say, "Have a good year." That is all.

I'm walking, yet each step is light. I have fasted all day, but I feel like I'm floating on air. Yom Kippur has opened a window in my heart. All day my heart stood on tiptoe as I fasted and prayed. The last shout of the *Neilah* prayers echoes in my ears. I am filled with the resolve that this year will be different. The *shofar* blast lifted up all our prayers. I feel awake inside and whole. I feel protected from anger, resentment and sadness. On this night I don't feel guilty.

I dance with my children around the room and sing, "Next year in Jerusalem." This day made me feel more complete.

Chapter Twelve
Do What You Can

The Perfect *Esrog*

It was *Erev Succos* and Reb Zaidel did not have an *esrog* for *Yom Tov.* This was unheard of because everyone in town recalled that Reb Zaidel always paid a small fortune to obtain the finest *esrog* available. There had been some trouble in his family this year, and Reb Zaidel did not have a spare moment to procure an *esrog* until today.

"Good Morning, Reb Shmaryah," he said as he entered the shop of the *esrog* dealer. "Do you have an *esrog* for me?"

"All I have right now, Reb Zaidel, are the ones you see here on the table. I know that you won't be satisfied with their quality. There are some dark spots on most of them and others are shaped a little funny. Perhaps you would do better to wait for this afternoon when I may get a shipment of real beauties."

"No, no, Reb Shmaryah," he insisted, "I'll take one of these here on the table."

"But, Reb Zaidel," protested the merchant, "you always make such a fuss about getting the perfect *esrog*. Why are you ready to settle for an ordinary *esrog* this year?"

"Each year," explained Reb Zaidel, "I can afford to be choosy. Now it is almost Succos and I'm afraid that if I wait for the perfect *esrog*, I may be stuck without an *esrog* at all" (*Give Us Life,* the Chofetz Chaim).

Everyone yearns to reach out when someone they care about is in a crisis. However, very few people actually offer concrete help. One reason is because they are waiting for a "better *esrog*" to come in. They wait for tomorrow, because perhaps tomorrow they'll know what to say when they call or write. They wait for tomorrow because tomorrow the person in crisis might call them and then they will know what to do. They wait for tomorrow because perhaps tomorrow someone will take them along when they visit and that will make it go smoother. They wait for the very best act of kindness rather than the one that feels a little uncomfortable. They want their endeavor to proceed smoothly and easily, and consequently they are left without an "*esrog*" — they don't take concrete action at all.

The fear of having a person in crisis tell us, "I don't want your help," causes us to hesitate. We postpone action because we are waiting to do the perfect thing to help, but we end up doing nothing.

None of us likes being rejected. We all have experienced failure in our various endeavors. The result was not the anticipated one. Memories of these setbacks often prevent us from helping someone we know well who is suffering. At such times we feel discouraged or inadequate.

Ella Katz experienced many trials and tribulations when her son was born with a cardiac problem. She encourages people to reach out with their hearts and their hands. She teaches us many vital lessons about the importance of approaching friends and family to help them in times of crisis.

"My husband's Aunt Barbara made a point of coming to see us, although it involved quite a bit of traveling. She had spent her fair share of time in the hospital with a sick child who had since made a beautiful recovery, *Baruch Hashem.*"

We spoke of the friends who hadn't come or called, as they "didn't want to be in the way." Then there were those who came to be there for her, who said, "I'm here. I don't know if this is a good time. I'll leave if it's not, but I'm here if you need me."

How many times do we fool ourselves into believing that we are doing a greater kindness by our non-appearance? Aunt Barbara taught me not to be afraid. "Call. Let the person know you care," she told me. "Tell her honestly that you don't know what to say or do. Tell her you want to be there for her." True, you face the possibility of what may feel like rejection. But, Aunt Barbara taught me, that doesn't matter. Be there, and be ready to stay or leave, whichever is the greater kindness at the time.

Throughout her book, *Heartstrings,* Ella gratefully describes every kind act, large and small, from which she benefited. She says of the *Bikur Cholim* apartment, "The walls themselves were *chesed.*" I do recommend that you read the book and discover the tremendous *chesed* that is happening every day. I want to focus for a few moments not on the major acts of *chesed* she describes but on the small gestures of friends who gave of themselves to make Ella's life a bit easier.

These are the things that each of us can do too, and they do make a significant difference.

There were friends who came to visit and quietly listened to her pain. One friend sat and said *Tehillim* at the infant's bedside; another went down with Ella during a procedure and hugged her as the baby cried. Someone babysat so she could go to a *shiur,* while someone else brought Chinese food to the *Bikur Cholim* apartment and celebrated the first night of Chanukah with her at 10 p.m. Little things, such as making her bed in the hospital's parent's room every time they visited or taking Ella out for shopping and errands, made a big difference.

Trust yourself. When you have a good idea and want to do a kind action, decide you will act. It isn't necessary to be perfect — you just have to be sincere. Be yourself. The more honest and spontaneous you are, the more your offer to help will be appreciated. Leave your fear behind you, and make that phone call, write that letter, pay that visit. If you wait, you may end up without having done anything.

It isn't helpful to ask, "Is there anything I can do?" or to say, "Just call if you need something." That leaves the person in crisis with the responsibility of deciding what might help and of having the courage to request it. Often the person you want to help can't think straight because of their crisis. They may also hesitate to request something specific. They might feel foolish asking for lunch or coffee when they are stuck at the bedside of a seriously ill person. If you really want to help you may need to take the initiative.

When you have a big problem or a friend is in trouble ask yourself, "What can I do to help in this situation?" Even small productive actions lessen our anxiety and help us feel that we will be able to cope with the problem in the long term. In the following interview Rochel discusses a difficult problem and how she was able to deal with it in a surprising way.

Interview

Roiza: Is there someone you respect from whom you learned to have faith in Hashem instead of worrying?

Rochel: Whenever I call my friend and ask how things are, no matter how tough the situation is, she says, "*Baruch Hashem* for that." Even when her husband lost his job, and they have eight children to support, she still said, "*Baruch Hashem* for that."

Roiza: People worry because they face an impossible problem and they just can't think of a way to solve it. What difficult problem did you have recently?

Rochel: When this friend's husband was fired I felt really concerned because now they would have to manage on one income. She called to ask, "Where can I buy a shoe rack?" As she described what she was looking for I felt bad that she should have to buy it since money was so tight. My first impulse was to just buy one for her, but I knew that she would feel embarrassed to accept a gift.

Roiza: You really cared about your friend, but you didn't think you had a way to help because she wouldn't accept a gift you bought. What happened next?

Rochel: Later that day I went to my mother-in-law. The exact shoe rack my friend had described was sitting there right on the sidewalk. The chrome didn't have a single scratch. It was the kind you put on the bottom of a closet. It was the right size. All I had to do was bend down, pick it up, and put it in the back of my minivan.

Roiza: You found exactly what you needed. It was truly a surprise. How did this experience help you find strength for your other troubles ?

Rochel: I felt that Hashem was telling me, "Of course I'll help you. Just do the best you can." We really grow by leaps and bounds when these things happen. I know Hashem takes care of my trivia. In this instance I felt that *I* am a messenger from Hashem.

Roiza: Why is it important to worry less and trust Hashem more?

Rochel: If we are consumed by concern over every little obstacle, until we overcome it successfully we cannot concentrate on our responsibilities to Hashem. We get carried away with different tasks and forget what our really important jobs are. I have told myself many times, "If the shoe rack situation was resolved why shouldn't everything I worry about work out?" Afterwards I am able to calm down and look for something constructive to do.

Chapter Thirteen

Terrific People

Let this concept penetrate, it will help get your attitude on track. You may not have pondered it before, but it's the truth. Your *neshamah* is the real you, it is your very essence. The gift in meeting terrific people is that they remind us of this truth. Let me give you some examples:

One of the participants in my workshops escaped from Lebanon in the 1970s. She described the power of the *neshamah*. "We had to walk for many days over dangerous steep mountains. We ran out of food. We had no shelter. We had to walk all night and we couldn't sleep. Yet we pushed on. When one is sure the body has absolutely no more strength, one's *neshamah* still possesses the necessary strength."

When faced with the trial of taking her infant overseas for open-heart surgery, Ella Katz said, "Hashem can do anything, but I wasn't sure I could." Your mind interacts with the real world. Your mind tries to convince you that the concrete facts before you are the entire picture. However, there is a small voice of hope that tries to penetrate your logical mind, if you only permit it. Herein lies the struggle that produces frustration and hopelessness. Listen to your *neshamah* — the real you — carefully. Ella looked for Hashem's guidance constantly and her faith gave her strength daily. When some small detail worked out she looked upon it as an encouraging Heavenly message. Whether it was the friends who helped her pack, or the doctor who sat behind her on the flight to America, or the Rav who came to the hospital to make *Havdalah* for her — every bit of help was Hashem telling her, "Yes, you can do it."

Your mind and your emotions are an important element. Yet your spirit is the true you. Even if your body and emotions are in pain they need not limit the full expression of the true you. Let me give you an example of what I mean.

Chedvah Silberfarb was struggling with a terminal illness. The grim medical prognosis determined that she had only a few days to live. Under these trying circumstances this was her request of her friends/visitors: "You're all lavishing me with attention. But how many candies can one person eat? How many flowers can adorn one room? I see that on our ward the patients get a lot of attention. But on the maternity ward there are young women who go home with their newborn infants empty-handed, without layettes for their babies. If I had the strength I would open up a *gemach* for infants' clothing right now, in the hospital. We can hang up a sign right here in my room and ask all my visitors to invest in a *mitzvah*."

Although her eyes were glazed with death's fever, her mind remained clear and unclouded as she patiently planned a complete recycling operation. No detail escaped her — from the wrapping paper and the personal note of congratulations on each gift item to the transatlantic passage of the clothing, to be equitably distributed in *Eretz Yisrael*. Ever a realist, Chedvah would comment to visitors at her bedside, "Other people in my situation take extra morphine. I take more *gemach*" (*A Narrow Bridge*, p. 161).

In spite of the destruction of her body, Chedvah spoke from her spirit and her words are inspiring and heartwarming. If she had allowed herself to dwell on her situation, she surely would have given up. Instead she allowed her spirit to emerge and transform her reality. She accepted her illness and lived on a higher plane, whole in spirit and searching for ways to confer kindness.

When we see what other people like us have accomplished, a voice within us whispers, "You can do it too." Examining the inspiring acts of others makes our ideals more concrete. This is a simple and powerful method to help you discover your path to greatness. From books we gain knowledge, but from people we learn how to live. Avraham *Avinu* spoke with Shem, Noach's son. Shem's example of kindness, changed Avraham's life forever, as the Midrash explains:

> If Avraham had not been jealous of those serving Hashem, he would not have acquired heaven and earth. When was he jealous? He asked Malkitzedek (Shem), "How (in what merit) did you go out of the Ark?" Malkitzedek replied, "In the merit of the charity that we did there." "What charity," asked Avraham, "was there for you to do in the Ark? Were there poor people there? Only your family was there, so for whom did you do charity?" "For the animals and birds," answered Malkitzedek. "We did not sleep; instead we served one after another all night." Thereupon Avraham said, "Had they not done charity for the animals and birds, they would not have left the Ark. Only because they did charity did they go out. If I do it with people, how much greater it is!" At that time he planted an *eishel* in Beer-Sheva. *Eishel* is an acronym for *achilah, shesiyah, leviyah:* eating, drinking, and escorting" (*Shocher Tov* 37:1, p. 28, *Encyclopedia of Biblical Personalities*).

The terrific people I will introduce you to in this chapter are giants. Physically they may be small in stature, but their *neshamos* are huge. They are able to listen to the small still voice inside themselves. Their *neshamah* gives them the strength to overcome pain and obstacles, accomplish herculean acts of kindness, and live sincerely according to a penetrating standard of truth. On explaining the words *elyon samta m'onecha,* the commentaries point out that it is possible to walk on this earth, yet live on a higher plane. It is possible to be constantly alert to Hashem's will. These people succeed in doing routine acts in an extraordinary way. I hope they will change your life forever.

CONFIDENTIAL KINDNESS

Our community has dozens of *chesed* organizations. There are teas and dinners and mailings. There are women who receive recognition and their names appear in the newspaper. There are others who will stand and be applauded by 500 women at a dinner. They will deliver a speech and urge us to give and share. They really deserve the honors. I know that all year they are up early and out late working hard for others. Yet I am personally inspired by the many ordinary heroines in our midst who are never the guests of honor. They do their kind acts quietly and no one knows their name. (All names were changed.)

Every morning Shaindy drives her car toward Fort Hamilton Parkway. Soon she is on the bridge leading to Manhattan. Three ladies chat in the back seat. Shaindy is on her way to work, but this is not a carpool. The three passengers in the back are going to the hospital for physiotherapy. She stops at the first place. Casually, she parks the car and takes a wheelchair from the trunk. She helps her passenger out and settles her comfortably in the chair. A few minutes later she is on her way with a cheerful wish of "Get Well!" She proceeds to render the same assistance to her other two passengers.

No one talks about Shaindy's kindness. She wouldn't want you to mention it. "I'm so glad I can do it. Others do much more than I do. I'm just giving someone a ride on my way to work."

Tovah is a wholesaler. She signs dozens of gift certificates each year. Some are requested by various organizations as a raffle prize. Many others, however, she simply gives to those who can't afford to pay. They take them to the store and make their selection. The store owner knows Tovah's certificates are as good as cash.

A mother of a young infant will come home tonight and find a blank envelope. There will be a fifty-dollar bill inside and the humble message, "Mazel Tov."

Another mother will answer the door and find a delivery van at her door. They will unload a case of diapers and ask, "Where should we put this?" When she asks who sent it — the delivery man will smile and shrug his shoulders.

You can tell a lot about a person by the way they react with children. Rivka Bald *o"h* is the only one whose name I didn't change. May her inspiration be a merit for her. We all miss her.

Last week my four-year-old daughter Etty was sitting at the breakfast table. She said, "When are we going to visit Rivkah?"

"You want to visit Rivkah?" I asked. "Yes, she was my friend," Etty said. "She knew what a little girl likes, she talked to me and listened to me and she even brought me a game."

I wasn't sure Etty really remembered. We had gone together to visit Rivkah, my neighbor in *shul* who had cancer, shortly before Chanukah. So I asked Etty which game. Etty answered, "The one with the numbers on it that my big sisters play with."

I remembered — during our visit Rivkah got up and I didn't know why. Slowly she walked to the kitchen. She held onto the handle of the white refrigerator with one hand and reached up for the Rummikub game with the other. She almost lost her balance, but she managed to stay on her feet. Then Rivkah brought back the game for Etty. Rivkah made every person feel wonderful. She saw the beauty in every individual.

There is kindness everywhere, but the considerate acts done in private have a tantalizing magic to them. These are people like you and me who wake up, eat three meals and go to sleep. However, their ordinary day or week is enhanced by sincere giving. And that makes all the difference.

Exercise

WHO ARE THE TERRIFIC PEOPLE YOU KNOW? HOW DO THEY INSPIRE YOU? HOW CAN THEIR ACTIONS BE A CATALYST FOR YOUR GROWTH?

_____

_____

_____

_____

_____

Actual Responses

NEIGHBORS

by Cipora Shazuri Weber

I live in a large apartment-building complex so I have several hundred neighbors. Some of them I have known for 23 years while others come and go. It's always a pleasure to see a familiar face and stop for a few minutes to exchange warm words. I really appreciate the neighbors on my floor. I feel truly blessed to know them. Four of them are older women who are always involved in acts of kindness. They go to the nursing homes, cook for others, and visit homebound invalids.

There is an elderly couple that I think of often. I will call them Mr. and Mrs. S. Frequently they sit together on the outside bench. I admire his long beard, pure and white, that seems to blend in with his spotless shirt. His large black *yarmulka* matches his black vest and pants. She wears a light blue duster and a lovely colorful turban that frames her pretty face. They sit together, side by side. Each one has a *Tehillim* in their hands. From time to time they look up and smile at each other through their mingled tears.

There are other things I admire about Mrs. S. No matter how sick she feels, she is always waiting downstairs at the entrance of the building for her husband. She greets him with a special smile reserved just for him. She does this three times a day. His face radiates a warm greeting in return. Then they walk into the house and go up the elevator together. I have seen her go down to meet her husband in this way for 23 years.

Their marriage must be very special. If I could be a fly for a while I'd take the opportunity to enter their home for unobserved lessons. I'd sit on the wall and listen to my neighbor's conversations. Meanwhile, I try to emulate what I witness from the outside. Through my smiles, good words and simple kind gestures, I am building my most important family relationship.

A FRIEND

I have a terrific friend. Since we were in high school Frumie always had time for me. No matter how busy she was, she would listen and chat. Frumie and I both have large families. Once, she came to visit from California for a week and stayed with us. As soon as she got up in the morning she'd come upstairs to chat with my kids. She was careful to give time to each of them. She made each child feel important. Last night she called from California and she specifically asked to speak with my daughter, Fraidy. She made her feel like she was an important friend of hers. Her warmth and caring is unique. I try to be like her in this respect whenever I think of her.

CONSIDERATE

Although this woman was widowed at the age of 37, her concern for her fellow human beings is phenomenal. When I was widowed two weeks before my daughter's wedding, she called me every single day. She insisted that I eat properly and nurture myself in small ways. More important is the fact that she almost commanded me, "Dolly, remember — as you behave at the wedding so will the *olam* behave."

She gave me the encouragement to smile, be happy and set a joyful tone at the wedding. My daughter and our guests were able to dance and be joyous because I could overcome my inner feelings and be "*mesamei'ach choson v'kallah.*"

Her considerate ways have inspired me for the past 11 years. Her concern is contagious because now I do what I can for other people.

A GRACIOUS HOSTESS

I live in an apartment house. My dear friend Reizel invited us into her home on Succos so that we could have a *seudah* with her, her husband, children and grandchildren. Although my friend has her own special diet (she is diabetic), she inquired about my husband's needs (he has a heart condition). Since it was hard for us to walk both ways she arranged for us to stay till nightfall so that she could drive us home.

My friend is also talented and creative. Once, at a meeting, she brought supplies for a craft project. She took out some cardboard and feathers from her bag. It looked like nothing but she showed us how to make beautiful pins. Some people make everyone's life nicer.

THE HAT

She walked into my weekly Torah class. I noticed that she was wearing a hat. Why is she wearing a hat? I wondered fleetingly, but, after all, it was a pretty cold day. At the next week's class she was wearing a hat again. I was curious. Today it wasn't cold. How do you ask someone if she has decided to cover her hair?

A few women came up at the end of class to comment or ask questions. We were talking about the courage it takes to change one's life because one knows it's the right thing and just decides to do it from now on.

Linda ventured, "I told my husband that this year for Rosh Hashanah I was getting a hat. He was calm. He thought I meant that I'd just wear a hat to synagogue for prayers. Well, since Rosh Hashanah I always wear a hat. I haven't taken it off."

There are countless ways my life would improve if I could muster the quiet courage and persistence that Linda has shown.

THE MECHUTANIM

by Gitty Kar

When my *mechutanim* arrived at our house to meet my daughter the first time I was extremely anxious. I was concerned about how we would appear to them. Our apartment was small and pleasant, but nothing fancy. Of course my son-in-law was already serious about my daughter and wanted his parents to meet us.

When they arrived they seemed nice. As they were leaving, my *mechutenesta* said to my daughter, "I can see why my son likes you." Her words gave me a glowing feeling of relief. She was kind and gentle.

The way she conducted herself that first day is how I know her for the last ten years. She is not a mother-in-law to my daughter, she is a mother. She is not an "in-law" to me, but a good friend whom I can call with a problem.

She doesn't see problems, only challenges. If she arrives at my daughter's home and the children are rowdy, she will pick up a book and read to them. If she sees things are not in order she will ask what she can do to help. She is a special person whom I try to emulate. Her kindness and calm manner make her a joy to be with. I wish everyone had her non-judgmental heart.

QUIETLY

by Malky Farkas Treitel

Quietly
he lived
his life.

Quietly
he helped
others.

Quietly
he
suffered.

After
he died
his deeds
spoke
for him.

TERRIFIC PEOPLE

by Malky Farkas Treitel

My mother
will always
hug, kiss and play
with her grandchildren,
no matter
how much pain
she has from her back.

With great personal cost
to herself,
she will always
come through
for others.

My mother
is strong enough
to act wrong,
even when
she is right.

With a
damaged spine
she stands
straight and tall,

because she
is always
holding on
to Hashem.

THE REAL THING

by Malky Farkas Treitel

When you share
the same
experience
with someone,
but you are
thinking more
about
their welfare
than your own —
then you really care.

Chapter Fourteen
One Type of Worry That Helps

While I observed my 14-month-old baby late one night, I recalled the security that I had once felt as a child. I had just returned from a wedding and I found that someone had put the baby to sleep upstairs in my bed. She is just two feet tall, a mere 24 inches, yet she was occupying my whole bed. My little one was sprawled out in a horizontal position, her arms and legs spread out. She looked comfortable and peaceful — like a little angel.

As I admired her serene appearance I felt a wave of nostalgia shower over me. My heart was full of imaginary questions to my baby: What are you dreaming about? What do babies think about when they sleep? Are you thinking about the little things that fill your day? Perhaps you are envisioning running to your father and having him pick you up in his strong arms. The world looks lovely from up there, doesn't it? Or perhaps you imagine riding in the car to new exciting places. You love sitting in your car seat as you wait for new things to discover. Possibly you are dreaming about playing a game or singing a song with all your sisters and brothers. You love it when they clap and sing and you always assume they are cheering for you.

My mother's heart prayed: "Little one, may your dreams in life always be pleasant and serene. May there never be any dark nightmares in your future."

I sat quietly next to Rochela and listened to the echo of my baby's calm heartbeat. I realized that as a young child, I too did not worry because I had faith — if there was a problem Mommy would pick me up and everything would be fine again. I might not have been able to explain such faith but I understood that I was protected. Now, as an adult I can explain trust and faith — but can I **feel** it? Do I feel *bitachon* in Hashem, similar to the way a baby feels secure in its mother's arms? I felt that I would gain many benefits if I worked on this idea.

David *HaMelech* says that he relies on Hashem and feels safe "*k'gamul alei imo,* like an infant in its mother's arms."

The *Pele Yo'aitz* explains that just as our children rely on us and therefore don't worry, so should we rely on Hashem.

"Look at your children and the people of your household. They don't worry about anything. They depend on their parents who are only people of flesh and blood like them. They don't worry about your problems. So too, we must surely rely on our Father in Heaven.

"When one feels that burdens and worries are distressing him he should throw his load onto Hashem" (*Pele Yo'aitz*).

The *Pele Yo'aitz* explains that if we worry about serving Hashem, we are supported from Above. When we think sincerely about our service to Hashem, we often receive encouragement and guidance in the least expected ways.

In the Midrash there is a parable that also teaches that Hashem takes care of our mundane worries when we worry about serving Him:

Two people had fields. One lived in Teveriah and had a field in Tzippori. The other from Tzippori had a field in Teveriah. They both struggled to manage their properties from afar. Finally they struck a deal with each other, "I'll care for your field and you care for mine." So too, fear of Hashem is on earth and everything else is from Heaven, as it says "All is in the Hands of Heaven except for fear of Hashem." Hashem says to us, "You take care of Me and I'll take care of you" (*Pele Yo'aitz — Tirchah*).

When we learn to trust Hashem with the mundane aspects of our lives we are guaranteed to find a weight lifted from our shoulders. Our daily lives will ease considerably. And yet there is a second aspect of this partnership to which we must pay attention. It is here that the principle, "You take care of Me, and I'll take care of you" comes into play. It is a principle to which we pay a great deal of lip service but one that is often difficult to put into practice.

The *Mesillas Yesharim* urges us to worry about the spiritual side of life. "One who rushes along without reflecting whether his way of life is proper or not is like a blind man walking on the side of a river. His chances of falling in are surely greater than those of his remaining unharmed."

Rabbeinu Bachya in *Chovos HaLevovos* tells us that worrying about our service of Hashem is a *mitzvah*. "For a while push away all of your mundane worries and worldly pursuits and concentrate with heart and mind only on serving the A–mighty. As one pious person said, 'A–mighty, my sorrow because I did not serve You properly removes from my heart all other sorrows. My concern that I'm far from You distances me from all other worries.' Through this prayer and these sincere feeling, Hashem will be happy with you and your *mitzvos* and help you in every way."

Many women have found that even a little bit of time spent on personal growth can profoundly change their lives. Learning a Torah book over the phone every morning for five to ten minutes a day can transform one's day. Here, Tovah shares her stimulating experience about learning and its benefits. Although it's just a few minutes, that time in the morning means a great deal to her.

Interview

Roiza: When do you have time to think about your goals each day?

Tovah: Every morning I learn the laws of *lashon hara* with a friend and we each describe a situation we had in the past day and how we handled it. This helps me remember to be careful with my speech in the day ahead.

Roiza: What specific goals do you have?

Tovah: We each take a two-hour period during the day when we will really be conscious of what we say. We resolved that there would be no slander, words of anger, or insults during that time. It's very hard to decide to change completely, but setting smaller goals makes the challenge possible.

Roiza: Do you think that the success during those two hours gives you the impetus to accomplish even more?

Tovah: The effort I put into those two hours makes me more conscious for the rest of the day. It's happened already that someone made me angry or wanted to gossip, and I glanced at the clock and thought, "Well, I can't now — my time isn't up yet." Once the time passes I find that since I waited already I can dismiss the temptation completely.

Roiza: What did you learn from your experience with the "two hours"?

Tovah: It's discouraging to try to change everything overnight. I just can't do it. (No one can.) However, when I try to work on one trait at a time change is possible and even likely to happen. I just choose one particular thing I want to improve and then review my actions regarding that aspect every day. After staying with the "two hours" goal for half a year I added a second goal. I try to do at least one extra kindness for someone every day. Now, when someone calls for help, instead of thinking, "I'm busy," I say to myself, "O.K. this will be the kindness for today."

Roiza: A lot of people would rather read an easy book than take time out to exercise their minds. What got you into it?

Tovah: Has it ever happened to you? You hear that the little girl who used to live next door is engaged. You go to a school reunion and realize you are the oldest one there; or you meet a former student of yours who now has three children. All these things make us aware that time is fleeting and there is value in time well spent.

Chapter Fifteen

Coping With the Afternoon Slump

FREEDOM
by Malky Farkas Treitel

*I am
in bondage
to the most
severe
slave master,*

Myself.

*Being both
slave and master,
I struggle
to gain
a master's control,*

*yet fail
in perfection
because
I am a slave
to my
impulses.*

Do you have any of these symptoms of afternoon slump?

Your makeup has faded. There are wrinkles in your skirt. Your clothes feel uncomfortable, damp and constricting. Your vision dulls and you feel pressure in your head that might become a headache. You alternate between walking inch by inch or running frantically in circles. Several self-defeating thoughts echo in your head such as, "I'm too tired. I need a big chocolate bar now. I have too much to do, and I don't know where to start."

You'll be glad to know that you are not alone. The majority of those interviewed felt a significant drop in their energy level sometime during the afternoon. These were some typical responses when I asked — "What do you say to yourself at 3:00 p.m.?"

- "I'm tired. I want to eat."
- "The day is over."
- "I had so many plans, but I didn't do half of them. Time goes fast."
- "I'm missing something. I have such a big headache. I feel empty."

You can adjust how you feel in the afternoon by improving your lunch. Your brain relies entirely on glucose to mobilize its millions of cells regulating daily thought processes. Skipping meals or eating meals that are empty of nutrients forces your brain to "run on vapor." Here are some nutritional guidelines to help you feel more vibrant in the afternoon.

1. Eat a moderate size, low-fat lunch, including carbohydrates and protein. Women appear to be more susceptible than men to carbohydrate-induced drowsiness, but anyone will be less alert and make more mistakes after a carbohydrate-rich lunch of pasta, for example, as compared to a turkey sandwich. Drs. Lieberman and Spring state that "It seems likely ... that carbohydrate relative to protein decreases arousal level and impairs performance" (*Food and Mood,* by Elizabeth Somer).

2. Drink Water. Chronic low fluid intake is a common but often overlooked cause of fatigue. Water is important for our health and our emotional well-being. It helps us think. You

aren't drinking enough if thirst is your only guideline. When you are busy or nervous you might not even remember that you are thirsty. Everyone needs 6-8 glasses of water a day.

3. Don't skip breakfast and eat a heavy lunch. Rav Nachman of Breslav said, "Eating bread for breakfast is good for controlling anger."

   "The morning meal stimulates the nervous system; it revs up hormones and neurotransmitters in the brain for an active day. If a person goes without a healthy breakfast and lunch, it's much more difficult to concentrate or get work done — making the day's tasks even harder" (Dr. George L. Blackburn, *Prevention*).

4. Limit rich or sugary foods. Yes, it's true that sugar makes you feel better for the moment, but that quick jolt is followed by a letdown and increased fatigue and nervousness.

   The *Rambam* wrote: "A person who eats sweet food to gratify his desires — even though the food will be dangerous to his health — is like an animal. This is not the behavior of an intelligent person" (*Shemoneh Perakim,* Ch. 5).

5. Snack Right — G–d provided us with a variety of nutritious foods of every taste and color. For an energizing snack try one of these:

   A. Bananas — Bananas are a good source of vitamin B6 and Potassium. Vitamin B6 deficiency causes fatigue, depression, irritability and reduced learning ability.

   B. Cheerios, raisins and a cup of yogurt — Yogurt is a good source of vitamin B2. Vitamin B2 deficiency causes irritability.

   C. Granola — The oats in granola are a good source of biotin. Biotin deficiency causes depression, fatigue and sleepiness.

   D. Rice Cakes — A bowl of brown rice is even better. Brown rice can help you overcome irritability, restlessness and fatigue.

E. Frozen fruit-juice bars and crackers

F. Baked Apple

G. Baby Carrots

Fruits and vegetables help protect you from cancer, heart disease, premature aging, fatigue and possibly memory loss. Everyone should be shopping more often at the fruit counter.

We all know that there's a connection between the quantity of stress we feel and the quality of our eating. Some of us can barely swallow when we are under pressure. On the other hand, some of us soothe ourselves with snacks like cookies, cake and chocolate. It's a mistake to rely on the counterfeit comfort of food instead of finding spiritual comfort.

Do you have a "spirit ache"? Do you feel overwhelmed and overworked? Are you relying on food to recharge your inner batteries? Instead invest a little time to get in touch with the essence of who you really are.

Rav Eliyahu Lopian says, *"Just as the body needs food, the soul needs sustenance. The foods for the soul are fulfilling the commandments, learning Torah and prayer. If one neglects the performance of a commandment, or doesn't do it properly, his soul will starve and become weak" (Lev Eliyahu).*

Rav Eliyahu Lopian elaborates and explains the verse, " 'I have created the *yetzer hara* and I have created Torah as a spice to counteract it.' " When one adds the 'Torah spice' to one's 'pot of life,' life takes on meaning and flavor."

I decided to explore the analogy of the "Torah spice." I was skimming through my Pesach cookbook when I realized that on Pesach we eat a plethora of potatoes. Potatoes are a very humble, unassuming vegetable — plain white inside, dull brown outside. Yet, somehow we have to exist on them for eight days. What do we add? A few spices and a little creativity. You can make fried potatoes, chicken-soup potatoes and layered potatoes (potatoes sauteed with layers of onions). The cookbook also featured latkes, kugel and knishes (you use fried eggs for the "pastry"). Then there are mashed potatoes, and golden mashed potatoes (add two carrots). Other possibilities are potato supreme, baked with a tangy lemon juice dressing, potato puffs, and stuffed potatoes with meat filling. Our family also enjoys potato-egg salad. It all adds up to 13 different ways to eat the same potato.

If you have a spirit-ache because life seems dull, drab and repetitious, add some spice and creativity. The simple, universal truth is that "Torah spice" can definitely rejuvenate your life. Be creative in finding new ways to apply Torah formulas to your routine. Creativity and "Torah spice" are easy, practical methods to turn your life around and set you in the right direction.

As one mother said, "After a meal I sit down and *bentch* out loud with a *bentcher.* I feel good about it. My children will remember that they saw me use a *bentcher* and not just mumble to myself."

This mother was adding some "spice" to the *mitzvah* of *Bircas HaMazon* by looking into a *bentcher* and saying the words audibly and clearly. A simple straightforward change of this sort can bring remarkable results. *Mitzvos* can work their magic in our lives and hopefully in the lives of the generations that will follow us.

Chapter Sixteen
Action Checklist

ACTION CHECKLIST

- ❏ I don't have enough time.
- ❏ If I can't do it perfectly I'd rather not do it at all.
- ❏ I often feel guilty.
- ❏ Opportunities slip through my fingers.
- ❏ I want to help others but I don't know what's needed.
- ❏ I can't stay with the goals I set.
- ❏ Everyone is so critical
- ❏ I wish I spoke less *lashon hara*.

How many of these sound like you? Let's see if you can improve the quality of your life with positive action. The following questions can help you motivate yourself. If the question interests you, turn to the corresponding pages to see more.

1. Do I feel I can accomplish many good things? (pages 119-120)

2. Do I feel that my actions can make a significant difference? (page 121)

3. What do I fear most? Why do I put off reaching out to others? (page 120)

4. What are the benefits of this fear? (page 120)

5. What would happen if I let go of this fear? (page 121-123)

6. I give myself permission to act in the following three ways:

a. _____

b. _____

c. _____

WORDS
HABITS
ACTIONS
THOUGHTS

Chapter Seventeen
Strength Through Prayer

WHAT IS PRAYER?

Every day gives us a new opportunity to find a deeper insight into the things we do. We look for a better way to perform a *mitzvah* and develop new concepts that will help us focus on our life's purpose.

I've gone through many stages with *tefillah*. There was a time when I said the Morning Prayers perhaps twice a week. Now I really try to pray twice a day and I succeed most of the time. Fridays are the hardest. Can I say that I have more time with five children than I had when I was a young newlywed? But I do have more worries.

The challenge is to turn to Hashem with the trust of a young child to a father. How many times do our children just have to tell us about a scrape or a bruise and once we have listened their pain eases and they rush off to play again. If you yearn to have the same lightheartedness then you must have complete trust when you speak to Hashem. You can truly come close to Hashem through prayer and become one with your spiritual self.

> Prayer — *tefillah* is related to the verb (used in Mishnaic Hebrew) *tofel*, to "attach," or "join," or "bind together," as two pieces of a broken vessel are pieced together to make it whole again.

Our soul is "truly a part of G-dliness," and it therefore longs to be reunited with G-dliness, just as a small flame when it is put close to a larger flame is absorbed into the larger flame. We may not be aware of this longing, but it is there nevertheless. Our soul has been called the "candle of G-d." The flame of a candle is restless, striving upwards, to break away, as it were, from the wick and body of the candle; for such is the nature of fire — to strive upwards. Our soul, too, strives upwards, like the flame of a *candle (My Prayer, pp. 6, 7).*

Parashas Vayeilech (31:18) — ...וְאָנֹכִי הַסְתֵּר אַסְתִּיר פָּנַי, *But I will surely have concealed My face ...*

HIDE AND SEEK

A chassidic Rebbe was sitting at his desk toward twilight. His son came running in. He was crying. Between sobs he panted, "We were playing hide and seek. Everyone went to hide. Then my friends left me hiding. They didn't come to look for me, they just left me alone. They went off to play a different game."

The Rebbe sighed. There were tears in his eyes. "My son, that's how it is between the Jews and Hashem. It's true we are in *galus* and Hashem is hiding. Hashem is waiting for us to search for Him, to learn more about Him and yearn to come closer. But we are too busy playing our games. We are distracted and we forget to seek Hashem."

Hashem is waiting for us. At this moment Hashem is waiting for us to begin seeking Him.

In *Yeshaya* Chapter 56 it says that Hashem will bring us to His House of Prayer. We learn from this that Hashem prays, but for what? Hashem prays that man should be inspired to pray to Him. Hashem arouses the desire in us to pray. Without this how could frail man approach Hashem? This is Hashem's gift to us.

Have you ever tried to contact the bank, electric company, police station, insurance company, or department store? It may be difficult to get through to all of these people, but Hashem's lines are never busy. Furthermore, Hashem is waiting eagerly for our prayers.

Try to keep this image in your mind. Remember it sometime today. Perhaps you might ask yourself, "What is Hashem waiting for now?"

In the time of the *Beis HaMikdash* a person would bring a sacrifice and before his eyes a fire descended from the Heavens and accepted his offering. If someone was puzzled by a profound question or had to make a difficult decision, he went to the prophet and inquired, "What does Hashem want me to do right now?" The prophet guided him.

In *galus,* Hashem appears to be hidden. There are many questions that don't have answers. One prays but doesn't know if his prayer was accepted. It's important for us to remember that although Hashem is hidden, He is constantly watching over us, as it says in *Shir HaShirim,* מֵצִיץ מִן הַחֲרַכִּים — "Hashem watches us through the cracks," i.e., the cracks in the Western Wall. What is meant by "Hashem is watching through the cracks"? When one is looking through a crack he can see you even if you cannot see him; Hashem is watching over us even though we cannot see Him.

Our *tefillos* are more energetic and vigorous if we pray with the inner conviction that Hashem is listening. We feel closer to Hashem when we concentrate on the meaning of the words and remember that we are talking directly to Hashem, our Father and King.

The *Maharal* of Prague asserts that not only do we feel closer to Hashem when we pray sincerely, but sincere prayer tangibly makes our life better.

"Hashem is just as responsive to a person as the person is responsive to Hashem. If you concentrate on prayer and do not turn away from Hashem, Hashem will be responsive to you completely" (Maharal of Prague).

Prayer should be very personal. I try to make a list before I begin, thereby reminding myself to pay attention to the specific things G-d helped me with yesterday and ask for His assistance today.

In our prayers we speak to G-d in three ways:

(1) We praise G-d for His wisdom and guidance as seen in nature and in history.

(2) We ask G-d to help us personally and also to redeem and help the entire Jewish nation, as well as all Mankind.

(3) We thank G-d for His assistance to our forefathers and to us personally.

THANKING HASHEM: WHY IS IT IMPORTANT?

We come closer to G-d by consciously focusing on the good in our lives and realizing that everything we enjoy is a gift from Him. As the *Ramban* states, "The intent of all the commandments is to bring us to gratitude to Hashem for having created us. This is the purpose of creation. Hashem's only desire for us is that we give thanks to Him, declaring, 'We are Your creatures'" (*Illuminating the Generations*, p. 167).

WHERE DID THE GRATITUDE ASPECT OF PRAYER ORIGINATE?

In the first 2,000 years after creation there were many people who spoke and prayed to G-d — recognizing His rulership of the world and asking Him for help. Adam, Noach, Shem, Avraham, Yitzchak and Yaakov all spoke to G–d and G–d spoke to them. It was a woman, however, who pioneered the concept of thanking G–d through prayer — the matriarch Leah, Yaakov *Avinu's* wife. Hashem told Leah through prophecy that there would be 12 tribes born to Yaakov's four wives: Leah and her maidservant and Rachel and her maidservant. Leah expected that each woman would bear three sons. When Yehudah, Leah's fourth son, was born, Leah felt that she had received more than her share and she declared, הַפַּעַם אוֹדֶה אֶת ה׳ — "This time I will gratefully praise [thank] Hashem" (*Bereishis* 29:35).

Our sages describe her contribution to the future of mankind: "From the day the Holy One, Blessed is He, created His world, no person expressed gratitude to the Holy One, Blessed is He, until Leah. She did so, as it is said, 'This time, I will gratefully praise Hashem.' " We learn two lessons from Leah:

1. She saw the good in her life and thanked G-d for it despite her troubles. Yaakov favored Rachel. Leah never succeeded in earning Yaakov's complete love and acceptance and this caused her much pain. Yet, she focused on the good in her life — the children G-d gave her.

2. We are called *Yehudim*. Our national aim is to emulate Leah and thank G-d as she did.

WHAT DOES GRATITUDE DO FOR YOU?

The prayer we say every morning as soon as we arise, the *Modeh Ani,* contains only 12 words. However, the impact of these words can sustain us through the entire day.

The Rebbe of Vorke quotes this verse from *Tehillim* (90:14): שַׂבְּעֵנוּ בַבֹּקֶר חַסְדֶּךָ וּנְרַנְּנָה וְנִשְׂמְחָה בְּכָל יָמֵינוּ — "Satisfy us in the morning with Your kindness, then we shall sing out and rejoice throughout our days."

We learn from this that if our mornings are filled with an awareness of the kindness of Hashem, we will be joyful the entire day.

One of my friends says "It's a beautiful morning" so often that her children have caught on. "It's not enough just to notice the good," she says. "You have to *embellish* the good. Enjoy every flower and every tree and every bird and thank Hashem."

I've often heard women say that they don't have time to pray. *Chazal* answer that if you give time to Hashem by lengthening your prayer Hashem will give you time — הַמַּאֲרִיךְ בִּתְפִלָּתוֹ מַאֲרִיכִין לוֹ יָמָיו וּשְׁנוֹתָיו (*Berachos* 54).

In his memoirs, *Go My Son,* Rabbi Chaim Shapiro describes an elderly Jew he met who lived by the principle that prayer is life!

> Suddenly, from behind a thick clump of bushes and low trees, I heard someone singing a *niggun.* I couldn't believe my ears. As I listened more carefully, I could make out the Hebrew words: "*El ginas egoz yo-o-raditee* ..." I made a mental note of where the *niggun* was coming from and hurried on to the office.

After delivering my message, I galloped off toward the clump of bushes. I caught a glimpse of a bearded man with a radiant face, sitting on the ground singing softly with his eyes closed. When he heard me approaching, he stopped singing and opened his eyes, eyes which seemed to pierce straight through to my soul.

I explained to him that I was from the railroad brigade, and was a former yeshivah student. "Look, I have *tefillin* here. I always carry them with me."

"*Tefillin!* For 15 years I haven't put on *tefillin!*" Tears rolled down his face. When he calmed down he told me that he was Nachman Baranow, a Breslaver *chassid.* He'd been convicted of teaching Torah to Jewish children and sentenced to 20 years in prison. For 15 years he'd been in a prison camp. Reluctantly I explained to him that I couldn't come the next day. He insisted that I give him detailed instructions as to how to get to my bunk. I begged him not to come, for he would surely be shot trying to leave the prison grounds.

The next morning, as I was finishing my morning prayers under my blanket, I felt someone touch me. I was terrified; I'd been discovered wearing my *tefillin!* I ripped off the one strapped to my forehead and stuck my head out of the blanket. In the dim light of dawn I recognized the white beard. "Reb Nachman! You escaped! You'll be shot!" I cried out. All the terror I had felt for myself seconds before became terror for his safety.

"*Sha!*" he whispered. "The guard is right outside. Let me have the *tefillin* — hurry!" He climbed into my bunk. Standing guard alongside, I heard sobbing under the blanket. I put my hand on the blanket. The cloth was soaked with his tears.

I heard someone outside and rushed to the door. A soldier was waiting there with a rifle and bayonet hanging from his shoulder. He was contentedly chewing on a piece of bread; Reb Nachman had bribed the guard with his food ration.

Soon, he was out of the bunk. "I'll see you tomorrow, at the same time." I begged him not to risk his life.

Choking with tears, he whispered, "Listen young man, for 15 years I haven't put on *tefillin*. Now that I have a chance, so what if I'll be hungry? You think this is the first time I've gone without food? They locked me up for seven days without food once because I wouldn't chop wood on Shabbos. *Baruch Hashem,* I'm still alive!"

הַמַּאֲרִיךְ בִּתְפִילָּתוֹ מַאֲרִיכִין לוֹ יָמָיו וּשְׁנוֹתָיו — "One who expands and prolongs his prayers will have his days and years prolonged." We understand that Hashem prolongs one's years by granting one a longer life. How does Hashem prolong one's days? Isn't every day as long as the one before it? Isn't every day exactly 24 hours long?

On some days we accomplish much more with our time. Everything flows smoothly. We get into the car and it starts immediately. We reach the train just as it's pulling into the station. There is no line at the bank. Our children are on time for the school bus. Everyone is healthy and in good spirits. Our supper is delicious and nothing burns.

On other days we "waste" time at every turn. One emergency after another suddenly arises. Our children miss the bus and our car won't start. There is a long line at the bank. Then we get a call from school that our child has a stomachache and wants to come home. It was the same 24-hour day, yet nothing seemed to flow.

In the merit of prayer our days truly are longer. We accomplish more because the hidden hand of Hashem is guiding us and helping us at every step.

Have you ever wondered what you can ask for when you pray? In *Sefer Mitzvas HaBitachon* (p. 21) Rabbi Shmuel Huminer reminds us that we should pray for anything we need. בְּכָל יוֹם וָיוֹם, וְכָל עֵת וָעֵת, וְכָל שָׁעָה וְשָׁעָה, עַל כָּל מַה שֶׁמִּצְטָרֵךְ לוֹ לְאָדָם בֵּין דָּבָר קָטָן, בֵּין דָּבָר גָּדוֹל, יִבְטַח בהקב"ה שֶׁיַּעֲזוֹר לוֹ עַל הַדָּבָר הַהוּא וְיַזְמִין לוֹ כָּל הִצְטָרְכוּתוֹ. — "*Every day — at all times, every hour — whatever needs you may have, be they something small or something major, you should trust that Hashem will help you with your request and provide you with all your needs.*"

RELY ON HASHEM'S KINDNESS

When I was four, I filled out one of my father's checks for $1,000 and gave it to him for a birthday present. My father laughed and said, "You can't write checks if you don't have money in the bank." This holds true for money, but fortunately, not for faith! When we pray, we can write "checks" even if there isn't any "money" in the account.

Depend on Hashem. It is best when one relies on Hashem's free kindness. However, one is not always sure that this will be effective; since he assumes he isn't worthy of free kindness, he doesn't honestly count on his prayers. That is why the request isn't granted. If he would honestly trust in G-d, G-d would not withhold His kindness. G-d always wants to give blessing to one who honestly trusts in Him (*Sefer Mitzvas HaBitachon*, p. 48).

PRAYING FOR OTHERS

One Monday afternoon at the *Tehillim shiur*, we discussed the importance of praying for others. Esther said, "At a lecture I learned that when a woman is giving birth it is a time that prayers are answered, like when a bride is under the *chuppah*. When my baby was born I mentioned the names of two people who didn't have children. Within a year they both had children." I began asking everyone I knew if they could suggest a source for this because I felt it was a fantastic concept. Imagine, when we are in pain we can do something wonderful with it! We can ask Hashem that it should be a merit to help those in need. Our pain can become a vehicle for blessing.

כְּאַיָּל תַּעֲרֹג עַל אֲפִיקֵי מָיִם כֵּן נַפְשִׁי תַעֲרֹג אֵלֶיךָ אֱלֹקִים — "As the deer call longingly for the brooks of water, so does my soul call longingly to You, O G–d" (*Tehillim* 42:2). The Midrash explains: "The deer possesses an anatomical peculiarity. Its womb is too small to allow for the birth of its young. During labor the helpless deer cries out in agony. Hashem has mercy on her and dispatches a snake to bite her. This sudden stab of pain causes a muscle spasm which opens her womb so that the fawn can emerge safely." The Midrash also explains, "The deer is the kindest and most devout of all animals. When the other beasts and animals are thirsty, they gather around the deer. The deer then digs a hole in the earth, inserts her horns and screams in anguish. Hashem takes pity on her and brings water."

The *Alshich* says that despite the deer's suffering and personal anguish she calls to Hashem to help *all* the animals.

Rabbi Mordechai Finkelman discussed this verse in *Tehillim* at a lecture. He said, "A tremendous merit is aroused when someone in pain prays for others. When we are in physical pain of any kind it's an opportunity to ask Hashem to help someone in need."

Mindy smiled and said, "I agree with Esther about the power of praying for others. You see, I didn't have children for many years. *Baruch Hashem* I have five children now. When my sister was in the hospital having a baby she prayed for me constantly. The doctor's were amazed that even when she was in pain, she screamed out a prayer for me. About a year later I had my first child."

We have discussed the many different thoughts we can have in mind when we are praying. Reb Simchah Bunim of Peshis'cha zt"l says that we should ask Hashem, "Help us to serve You better. May our actions today give You *nachas*." This is the highest level of prayer. Reb Bunim explains with a parable:

There was a king whose son rebelled and was banished to a peasant village. Although the king didn't visit his son he sent agents every month to observe his son and to assure the king that he was safe and in good health. Several years passed. The king felt an overwhelming longing to be reunited with his son. He thought, "If he would only apologize and sincerely want to return to the castle I'd bring him back to me now. However, he must at least want to return, I won't force him."

The king decided to give his son a chance to return. He sent the prime minister to the peasant village with a message,

"Your father is prepared to bestow upon you whatever your heart desires; make a wish and it will be fulfilled." The king hoped that the son's request would be, "Father, I want to be with you."

The prime minister found the prince at work tending the sheep in the distant village. Enthusiastically he informed the prince of the king's magnanimous offer. "You can have whatever your heart desires ..."

The prince thought for a moment and said, "I could use a nice sturdy home. The walls of my hut are cracked in some places and the roof leaks. I would also like a warm fur coat."

We underestimate the power of our prayers. All of us can call to Hashem just the way we are — with our minds, our hearts and our abilities. We don't have to wait to be different or better. We can call out to Hashem now. We should beg to be reunited with Hashem in Yerushalayim. Instead we merely ask for a nicer house, a better livelihood, some more conveniences ...

The following true story (which I heard personally from the *baal tefillah*) will inspire us to *daven* more sincerely. These are his words:

It was two weeks before Rosh Hashanah. At two a.m. the phone rang. My friend had startling news for me. After 70 years the Russian government had agreed to allow the *shul* in Lvov to open its doors again. Then came a question I will never forget. "We need someone to lead the Rosh Hashanah prayers. Do you think you could go to Russia for Rosh Hashanah?"

I hesitated. It was such a surprise. I didn't know what to say. I said I'd call back.

I talked it over with my wife. She said, "Of course you should go. How can you turn them down?" So I called back and said, "Of course we'll go."

I have been a *baal tefillah* for many years, but this time things were different. Many more people attended than had been expected. Some people had been on trains for 20 hours to attend these services.

Although the room was packed, only about a dozen old men in the front row knew how to *daven*. The rest of the people just listened. I wanted everyone to feel that they were a part of the *tefillos,* but they didn't know what a *berachah* was or when one begins and ends. I said, "When I raise my hand say *Amen.*"

After *Shacharis* I spoke for a few minutes. There was such a feeling of intensity in the room. These people cared so much, yet knew so little. I felt I just had to say something encouraging.

I told the story of Rav Levi Yitzchak of Berditchev and the Cantonist soldier. The soldier didn't know how to pray, so he said the *aleph beis* and then said, "Master of the Universe — please accept the *aleph beis* and You form these letters into the prayers." Then Rav Levi Yitzchak told all the congregants that the simple, sincere *aleph beis* of the Cantonist soldier had insured them all a good year.

I finished the story. And then in halting English someone called out. "Rebbe, we too want to say *aleph beis.*" There was a loud chorus of voices. "Please Rebbe, say *aleph beis* with us!"

So I said, "*Aleph,*" and hundreds of voices repeated "*Aleph.*" I said "*Beis*" and there echoed a loud response — "*Beis ...*" By the time I reached "*Hei*" we were all crying.

I've *davened* in many *shuls,* but I'll never forget that Rosh Hashanah in Lvov.

Exercise

Think of times when you called out to Hashem and your request was granted.

Actual Responses

1. I went to *Eretz Yisrael* this past summer and prayed at the *Kosel* every day to find my *zivug* and merit to build a true Jewish home. In our society once you reach the age of 21 you begin to get nervous. When I came back from *Eretz Yisrael* I felt alone. I longed for the feeling I had when praying by the *Kosel.* When I visited my grandmother her friend stopped in. My grandmother mentioned that her friend was

going to *Eretz Yisrael* next week. I took two dollars out of my pocketbook, hastily wrote my name on a piece of paper, and said, "Please, could you mention me when you go to the *Kosel* and give this money for *tzedakah* there."

A month later I met Chaim. We saw from the start that we had a lot in common. I'm getting married in March. Of course, my grandmother has been busy sharing the exciting news of my engagement with all her friends. The friend I met at my grandmother's house called to wish me *mazel tov*. "I just want you to know that I prayed for you not only by the *Kosel* but at every one of the holy places that I went to in *Eretz Yisrael*. *Mazel tov* and may you have only happiness."

2. My neighbor didn't have children. When I was in my ninth month she gave me her name and her mother's name. "Please pray for me," she asked. During labor I mentioned her name over and over again. She had a child that year.

3. For a while I went to a school where one other girl and I were the only observant girls in the class. She once explained to me why her family keeps Shabbos. "Before I was born my parents didn't have children. My mother promised that if she has a child she will keep Shabbos. My mother had me and my brother. Now of course we keep Shabbos."

Chapter Eighteen
Shortcuts to Happiness

We always have a choice. We can choose love over hate, peace over conflict, happiness over depression, and gratitude over complaining. Each time we make these choices we enter Hashem's presence. As King David said in *Tehillim*: בֹּאוּ שְׁעָרָיו בְּתוֹדָה חֲצֵרֹתָיו בִּתְהִלָּה — "Enter Hashem's gate with thanksgiving, His courts with praise" (*Tehillim* 100:4). Our heart is like a landscape. If we plant seeds of joy and gratitude, inner peace and success will grow.

This book has given you at least 40 tools for taking charge. Find the ones that suit you most naturally. It's time to replace stress with celebration, and years of questions and doubt with reliance on Hashem. We are all fully equipped; we have only to exercise our inner self.

Over the years I have had many opportunities to observe and interact with people who have consciously moved toward happiness. I've noticed some definite character traits that happy people share and tend to maximize. These varied "shortcuts" can make the experience of happiness more accessible, easier and, in some cases, instantaneous.

Since the aim of this sharing is not to fill our cups as if they were empty, but to bring what we know to the surface, some of the following ideas will probably appear obvious and familiar. If you've thought of one of these shortcuts on your own that's wonderful! It's a reassuring sign that you have come a long way in the battle with stress. Sometimes we search for complex remote ways to resolve problems while the obvious solutions have been overlooked.

SHORTCUT #1
FOCUS ON HAPPY, LIGHTHEARTED MEMORIES

Bringing happy thoughts to the center of the stage can make a significant difference. Lightheartedness chases away stress. Although this may seem obvious, in practice we rarely take even five minutes to think about our past pleasant experiences. On the other hand, memories of past failures seem to haunt us quite often.

Take time to think about things you have enjoyed doing. As one workshop participant said, "Last week, my two grandchildren came to visit. One put her dolls on the couch and the other put her dolls on the easy chair. I walked into the dining room and laughed. Then I sat down and told them how I used to play house with my sisters when I was a child and also used the easy chairs in my house. We even played house all together for a while."

Helena Jakobovics wrote about a calming childhood memory. I find that reading it is especially soothing because I also played under the dining-room table.

CHILDHOOD MEMORIES

by Helena Jakobovics

The house is one of a row of brick houses, warm and comfortable. It had two children's bedrooms and a master bedroom upstairs. The bathroom had lots of peach and black tiles and if you took a bar of soap you could write on the black tile as though it were a chalkboard. The stall shower was scary to me as a little girl. The space was small and the door had to be shut tight so that no water would leak out, and the shower water would come down with lots and lots of pressure.

Downstairs there was a small entry hall with a coat closet. If I opened the front door at a certain angle. I could enclose myself and my friends as though in an elevator. The living room had gray carpeting and furniture with flowers and a gray background to coordinate with the rug. The wallpaper, too, was on a gray background. There were casement windows overlooking the front porch and a built-in radiator that ran the length of the windows.

Sometimes I would pull a chair up to the radiator — probably not in the dead of winter when it was blazing hot — and sit in front of it playing an imaginary piano.

The dining room had a large mahogany table. The legs were enormous and there seemed to be mahogany bridges connecting these huge elephant paw legs. I would use one of these bridges as a pillow under my head and stretch out on the oriental-looking and immaculately cleaned and vacuumed rug to rest or read or think or whatever.

TRY

Try to use your imagination to achieve a calm feeling. Thinking about a favorite place can help you relax at this moment. This is more effective when you are specific in your thoughts.

SHORTCUT #2
REMEMBER WHO YOU ARE

Remember who you are. Remember to be distinctly yourself. Remember that you are a precious individual. Remember that it is a privilege to be a Jew and serve the A–mighty. As we say each morning, "But we are Your people, members of Your covenant, children of Avraham, Your beloved, to whom You took an oath at Mount Moriah, the offspring of Yitzchak, his only son, who was bound atop the altar, the community of Jacob, Your firstborn son, whom — because of the love with which You adored him and the joy with which You delighted in him — You named Israel and Yeshurun ... We are fortunate — how good is our portion, how pleasant our lot, and how beautiful our heritage!"

The Bobover Rebbe, *shlita,* stood up. The hall was quiet. The Rebbe looked around the room. He noticed the many tables that were covered with sparkling white tablecloths. The Rebbe saw the table settings and the plates filled with traditional *Melaveh Malkah* food.

The Rebbe saw hundreds of pairs of eyes of devoted *chassidim* looking up at him and waiting. The Rebbe began to speak. "Tonight, Hashem gave me a wonderful gift," the Rebbe, *shlita,* said.

"In order to explain it I have to tell you about my life 50 years ago in the middle of World War II. I lived outside the ghetto and possessed a set of papers certifying that I was a gentile. I was dressed in a Nazi uniform. My Polish name was Stanislav Lasky." The Bobover Rebbe paused and chuckled, "None of you sitting here today would have recognized me. Sometimes a Jew in the ghetto would cross the street to avoid me. I spent every waking moment trying to save a *Yid's* life. There was this coal-truck driver, all week he worked for the *Wehrmacht.* On Tuesday he worked for me. On Tuesday he delivered coal to the Hungarian border. He also delivered something else — Jews escaping from the ghetto. We built a false bottom in the truck. There was about a foot of space. The Jews were slipped inside like you would slip matzos into an oven. They had to lay motionless as the truck traveled to the border.

"I was sitting at a bar on the Hungarian border. I was waiting to meet my friend, the Polish peasant guide who would escort a group of Jews through the woods and mountains from Poland to Hungary. The bar was small. The room held a few stools and some bare tables. I noticed a young peasant boy sitting in the back.

"The boy looked up and our eyes met. We had recognized each other. It was Meir, a boy I knew well. He used to attend our yeshivah. He was also pretending to be a gentile. He came over to me and I took his hand in mine.

" 'Meir,' I said. He nodded. 'Meir, now there is a war and we are struggling to survive. Now I look like a Nazi soldier and you look like a peasant farm boy. I'm sure however that the war will end. Remember, Meir, remember. Remember that you are a

Jew. Your father and your mother were upright Jews. As soon as you are able, remember that you are a *Yid*.'

"Tonight before the ceremony a mature man with a long gray beard came up to me. I looked at him and he looked at me. 'Rebbe, I remembered,' he said.

"'Meir!' I called out happily. 'Rebbe, I remembered,' Meir said. 'I have several children and two dozen grandchildren and they are all upright Jews.' "

TRY

There is no limit to this story's message. It deepens and grows as you think about it. Try planting these words. Let them deepen and grow in a lovingly tended garden.

SHORTCUT #3

When you are feeling tense, ask yourself: Are my present thoughts A.S.K.?

A — appreciative

S — secure

K — kind

A — APPRECIATIVE. Refer to the chapter on appreciation, and if you begin to keep a *Baruch Hashem* Book it will help you to read it and add to it when you feel tense. It's important to appreciate the basics.

Every morning we thank Hashem for the ability to see. Indeed, it's wonderful to be able to see even something tiny. It's a pleasure to see color. Recently I heard Ariella Savir, a blind mother who has composed at least 20 song books for children, speak on a tape. She said, "Every morning I thank Hashem for the gift of sight. Seeing isn't just being able to see a flower physically. Seeing is the ability to observe and appreciate Hashem's kindness."

S — SECURE. It's hard to find secure thoughts when you are faced with problems. Sometimes one can't even think straight.

The mind swirls with unanswered questions and worries. However, if one habitually thinks Torah thoughts he develops a secure foundation and these healthy thoughts help him overcome life's trials and pain.

Yosef *HaTzaddik* personifies a person with a secure foundation. At the young age of 17 he was alone in the land of Egypt. This land threatened Yosef and his values. Nevertheless, he stood firm in his Jewish values and succeeded. He had a secure foundation from his father Yaakov's home.

A participant at a lecture described her grandfather, Rabbi Kassin *zt"l*. This was a man with a secure foundation. The problems and pain of life didn't overwhelm him. "My grandfather was the chief rabbi of the Sefardic community here in America. He was 95-years-old. He had minor surgery. When they brought him to his room he had five tubes attached to him, but his face was serene and peaceful. He said thank you to every nurse, doctor and person who walked into the room. On his first day home I went to visit. 'How are you?' I asked.

" 'I have pain, but nothing hurts me,' he replied.

"This I didn't understand, 'How can it be that the pain doesn't hurt?' I asked him.

" 'Because I am too busy thinking about the *Mashiach* to think about the pain,' he smiled.

" 'Tell me about the *Mashiach* so I may also feel this calm,' I pleaded.

" 'Bring me a piece of paper,' " he said.

"He took the paper and folded it up very small. 'This is Yerushalayim now,' he said. 'But when the *Mashiach* comes all the Jews in the world will come to Yerushalayim and it will grow like this.' He then unfolded one crease at a time as he enumerated each different group of Jews that will come to Yerushalayim. While he unfolded the paper he slowly described the wonderful peace and unity that will envelop the world. 'Each Jew will have his own palace, with hundreds of servants, and gold and silver will cover the streets ...'

"After that visit the entire picture I had of my life changed. I realized that I complain because I think only of my own little world, like the paper when it was folded up so small. I learned that I have to think about the big piece of paper that I saw at the end. I am a Jewish daughter, Hashem's child, and I'm part of a big plan."

K — KIND. Cultivate kind thoughts about others. Give people the benefit of the doubt. When Hashem examines us He wants to know if we have been kind in our judgments. He will be kind to us if we treated others accordingly. Habitually being kind in thought and action is a potent skeleton key. It opens the gates of Heaven.

Rav Huna, son of Rav Yehoshua, was in a critical state; his condition grew worse by the hour. Rav Huna lay motionless in bed, his eyes tightly shut; there was no sign of consciousness. Rav Pappa, his close friend, entered. He wept silently by his friend's bedside.

"How is the patient?" asked Rav Huna's disciples when Rav Pappa left the room.

"Make the necessary arrangements for the funeral," ordered Rav Pappa quietly.

Several days passed and to everyone's supreme joy, Rav Huna miraculously recovered. Those who had heard Rav Pappa predict Rav Huna's death took courage to ask, "Why did you think that we should prepare for Rav Huna's death?"

Rav Pappa replied, "When I told you that Rav Huna was about to die, this had truly been decreed by the heavenly court. But at the last moment, before the sentence was executed, Hashem said, 'Leave Rav Huna be. Just as he overcomes his feelings and forgives those who wrong him, so shall we overlook the letter of the law — his death sentence — and be bountiful towards him.'"

Because of his forgiving character Rav Huna was granted additional years of life (*Tales from the Gemara,* p. 27).

Chapter Nineteen
Reminding Yourself

Reading a book for the first time is an adventure, a search for the unknown. You are browsing through new possibilities. I hope this book has given you a different perspective. You see now that worry isn't inevitable; there is always another, more beneficial way to look at life.

This book's objective is to help us comfort and encourage ourselves. On all levels we can nurture our *neshamah*. Every small triumph in achieving closeness to Hashem and closeness to our family and friends is a tremendous victory. Every area you master, as you learn the new skills in this book, can be yours for a lifetime.

As the saying goes, "Life goes on." You can feel inspired and strong one day, but the next day your reality will be second-rate. Nurturing your spirit is an ongoing process. How can your new skills become a part of your life? How can you help yourself when you feel overwhelmed by worries and stress?

Don't forget your inner self. Remember every day that you are worthy because you were created in Hashem's image. No one can fulfill *your* mission or take *your* place in the world. There will never be another you in this period in history, born to these parents, in this country, in this city. Today is a precious gift that will come just once.

What can you do to remind yourself to feel peaceful inside despite the pressures you face?

PERSONAL TREASURES

Personal treasures are mementos that are meaningful to you. You carry them in your purse or put them in your car or in strategic places around your home. Of course grandmothers will always smile and relax when they see a photo of their grandchildren. One possibility is to carry a photo of someone you admire. Sometimes, looking at their picture helps you ask yourself, "What would this person that I admire do now? Can I do it too?"

Some other personal treasures are souvenirs from places you visited, a tiny *siddur* or *Tehillim,* anything that belongs to someone precious to you, or a piece of jewelry.

It helps to change treasures now and then so that they don't become so familiar that they are no longer special and as a result you forget to notice them.

STORIES

Why do our *mitzvos* become routine? What can we do to revitalize our feelings in our service to Hashem?

Rabbi Ezriel Tauber points out that *mitzvos* probably become mundane because of the demanding nature of living as a Torah Jew. He compares it to going on a long trip: Before departing you study a map and take note of all the different roads and highways you will have to take. Once on the road, however, you need to stay alert, watching out for the appropriate signs and exits. Periodically, though, it is necessary to look at the map and remind yourself where you are and where you have to go.

On the highway of life, too many of us often forget to do the latter. We are so busy with the road immediately in front of us that we tell ourselves we don't have time to stop, pull over to the side, take out the map and make sure we are not on the wrong road.

Practically speaking, what does it mean to look at the map? You have to work on developing your life's philosophy through Torah books and Torah classes. On a daily basis taking five minutes to read an inspiring story can enhance and guide everything you do. The clearer and more complete our personal outlook, the better we can relate to the specifics of our daily lives.

When you read a story about a Torah sage, ask yourself, "How can I apply this ideal to my daily life?" When you read a story about a mother like you who did something you admire perhaps you'll ask yourself, "If she can do it — why can't I?"

Collect your favorite stories, quotes and affirmations. Collect your family's stories. Tell your children about your ancestors and at the same time remind yourself that your goal is to emulate them. The next section in this book is a collection of uplifting anecdotes and stories. Enjoy them and may they inspire you to begin your own collection. Finally, I hope they facilitate your review of the basic reassuring beliefs that you have learned.

PART TWO:

Uplifting Treats for You

Uplifting Treats for You

STORIES TO HELP YOU ENJOY THE SIMPLE PLEASURES OF LIFE

FIRST DAY OF SCHOOL

On the first Tuesday of September, I held my seven-year-old son's trusting hand as we walked to school. My heart was filled with prayers and worries for him. As we walked I wished him success, health, wisdom and happiness. He answered, "*Amen*, but Mommy please don't bless me so loudly."

On the way home I met a neighbor. She had also walked her son to school. "I feel so happy," she said. "It's an enjoyable gift that we can take our children to yeshivah." I was surprised. I had not thought of it that way.

I said with a chuckle, "One day I might even take a grand-child to school."

Then with a smile my neighbor said, "Let me share something with you. Last year when my daughter in Israel had a baby, right at this time of year, I went to Israel to assist her with the older children. On the first day of yeshivah I took my grandson to school. The sun was shining. I felt that this was a glowing day. Suddenly the verse from *Tehillim* (115:18) came to my mind, 'And we will bless Hashem ... forever.' I thought, 'Hashem, through my children and grandchildren I can bless You forever.' I felt so grateful at that moment."

My neighbor walked on, but she has given me a precious gift. Walking my children to school or picking them up is no longer an ordinary chore for me. It's a occasion for gratitude to Hashem.

TRY

Try asking yourself from time to time, "How can I enhance this ordinary moment? How can I make this an occasion for gratitude to Hashem?"

PRIVACY

Did you ever wish you could pray in private? Would you like to go to a *shul* where you know no one and no one knows you? You can sway and cry and you don't have to talk or socialize. You aren't tempted to look up when you hear the door open because you don't know anyone. There are no distractions. It is only you before Hashem.

For several years I went to the *vasikin minyan* (a *minyan* that prays at sunrise) on Rosh Hashanah. I woke up at 6:30 and *davened Shacharis* at home. At 7 I left for *shul* and arrived for *Krias HaTorah*. The *shofar* blowing was at about 8 o'clock. I stayed for most of *Mussaf* and left at 11. In this way I was able to concentrate and calmly hear the *shofar*. I was also able to peacefully daven *Mussaf* in *shul*. I wasn't anxious about when my younger children would start becoming restless and make noise. Afterwards I brought all the children to listen to the *shofar* at our regular *shul*. My oldest daughters stayed for *Mussaf* while I went home.

We should be able to *daven* without being distracted wherever we are. When we sit among friends, family and acquaintances we should be able to express our emotions freely when we pick up the *siddur*. The opinions of others shouldn't make a difference to us. Yet I took the prayers more seriously at the *vasikin minyan*. It wasn't until I actually woke up early and prayed at this *shul* that I was aware of the difference. It was very intense, yet simultaneously relaxed. I was aware of a quiet simplicity inside.

You can feel all your feelings, cry all your tears, and crumple all your tissues — and it's fine.

You can be serious. You can be happy. You can be quiet. You can point to each word. You can bow for a few seconds longer. You can lift the *siddur* and cover your face. It's all fine. No one is looking because no one knows you. It's just you before the Master of the Universe.

Sometimes it's suitable to be a "tourist" in a *shul*. It feels good to go to a place where you can be your real self.

TRY

Can you take on the challenge of *davening* at a 7 o'clock *minyan?* Would your *davening* be different in a *shul* where no one knows you?

I COULD BE BETTER IF ...

I could be a better mother if I decided to be a happy and content parent exactly the way I am. I'd like to decide that being a loving mother is enough. I could decide that smiling as I serve supper, and sitting down at the table to hear their *berachos* and answer *amen,* and listening to their day is enough. Also, listening to stories, and pretending I never heard them before or answering homework questions and afterwards playing a board game could be enough. What if I decided that baking cake and *challah* and giving my child a piece of dough to make her own *challah* is sufficient? I need only decide that patiently testing a child in spelling, discussing the vocabulary words so another child will remember them better, and listening to my son read 42 *pesukim* of *Chumash* is enough.

However, I'm always thinking that I could be doing something more. I always want to get out and do something "worthwhile and exciting." I want to organize all the closets. I want to pair up all the socks. I want to save or earn a little more money. When there is a sink full of dishes waiting at night and my child says, "Mommy, please read me a story," what should I decide to do? What is more important? Am I properly enjoying what I already have? If I could answer these questions honestly I would surely be happier.

TRY

Try to spend five minutes making a list of things you enjoy that don't require spending any money. As the saying goes, "The best things in life are free."

MESSAGES THAT COUNT

Rabbi Avigdor Miller emphasizes that our first responsibility is to work on our personal growth. We learn this from the beginning of *Parashas Noach* where it says, "And these are the children of Noach, Noach was a righteous person." Rabbi Miller explains that the first child of Noach was himself. He cultivated his character, developed his wisdom, and refined all his traits.

In studying our past we find tools for present and future self-development. These are messages that we carry with us every day of our lives. Someone said that actions speak louder than words. My father doesn't speak much but his messages are heard even without words.

IS IT IMPORTANT?

My father's actions teach me to have priorities. Keeping calm is easier when you know that very few things that upset our daily routine have lasting significance. I grew up remembering that my father spanked me just twice in my life. Once because I tried to insert a foreign object into an electric outlet and the other time when I ran into the street.

My father's patience and gentle smile the 1,000 other times I vexed him carried a message. The message is one I strive to remember when others upset me. I can hear my father's wise counsel — "Is it really so important that you should lose your serenity over it?"

IT WILL HEAL

I entered the dining room. My father was sitting on the recliner. His hand was bandaged from the elbow until his finger tip. In an accident at the machine shop where he worked, the top of his finger was cut off. I was shocked, but my father was calm. "How are you managing? It must hurt so much!" I exclaimed. My father replied with confidence, "It will heal!" Whenever I mentioned his finger in the next month that was his answer, "Roiza, it will heal."

When I get caught up in self-pity over aches, pains, bruises, colds and flu, I remember my father's message. "It will heal."

A GOOD NAME

My father was working hard to perfect a new machine. I rushed in to the shop after school. I noticed that his hands were black with machine grease. "Wow, you sure got your hands dirty today!" I exclaimed. My father held out his hands and said with a smile, "These hands are clean. These are honest hands. They have never touched a dollar that belonged to someone else. When I meet a customer he greets me with a smile. A good name is the most valuable thing you can acquire."

The lessons my father taught me are ever-present. They have impacted my life significantly because they remind me of vital ideals and my ability to maintain those ideals. Each person must explore his or her own memory for meaningful lessons.

TRY

At the end of the day try to think about someone you admire. What lessons did you learn from them that you can use in your life now?

A CHILD'S RIGHTEOUSNESS

Children are naturally pure and righteous. They do the right thing with all their heart. They aren't always looking sideways to see people's reactions. A four-year-old sings about Rosh Hashanah. She sings about dipping the apple in the honey and a good sweet year. She believes with her whole heart that God will give us a good sweet year. Then she takes some coins and puts them in the *pushka* and prays for every member of her family. She has such confidence that G–d is listening!

A baby takes a *siddur* and sways. He can't read and doesn't know if he's holding the *siddur* right side up or upside down, but he knows that his family prays so he does too.

A child's high-pitched clear voice pronounces a *berachah*. We all answer *amen*. The child is happy that he can simply say the *berachah*.

A three-year-old boy receives a pretend *sefer Torah* as a gift for his *upsherin*. He hugs the Torah tightly. He wants to absorb its holiness with all his being. He loves the Torah simply and completely.

Children can talk to G–d and they know deep inside that G–d is listening. Children are righteous because they are not yet weighed down by everyone's conflicting values and ideas.

TRY

How about bending down the next time you talk to a child and communicating with him at his eye level? Derive inspiration from a child's pure soul.

COFFEE, TEA AND ME

I was fifteen years old. My parents were upstairs relaxing after a hard day of work. I was doing my homework in my favorite spot — the dining-room table. I sat surrounded by books, papers and spiral notebooks. Occasionally I jumped up to pull a *sefer* out of the shelf to answer a homework question. I heard my parents call, "Roiza, can you bring us each a cup of tea."

I went to the kitchen and took out the tray and glasses. I knew my father liked his tea stronger. My father liked two spoons of sugar, while my mother wanted only one. I measured out the sugar and put the tea bag in my father's cup first while the water boiled. The teakettle whistled. I let it whistle for a minute. My father likes the tea really hot. Then I poured the two cups of tea. I smiled as I walked slowly up the stairs. How easy this has become. I used to be afraid of the kettle. I used to have to take up only one glass at a time, because the tray was too heavy. Now I can carry the two steaming glasses of tea with confidence.

It is many years later and I'm upstairs resting in bed. My daughter goes to the kitchen sink and turns a knob. The automatic boiled water pours over the strawberry flavored herbal tea bag. She adds one and a half spoons of sugar and carries the disposable cup up the stairs. "Mommy, I just knew you needed a cup of tea," she says with a smile. So much has changed, yet so much is the same.

TRY

Why not share a childhood memory with someone you care about ...

BEAUTY

She called last night and her voice was beautiful. Her voice sang with joy and wonder. Her voice gave me a feeling of hope. I listened to her speak and I felt G–d's love and presence.

"*Baruch Hashem*, my son is six weeks old," she said. "He is so beautiful. I think he's beginning to smile at me. I'm so grateful. He is a true comfort."

Last year at this time Pessy had a baby girl. The baby was born with serious heart defects. When I spoke to Pessy last year her voice was sad and worried. The parents had to make many difficult decisions for which there were no clear answers. Which doctor? Which surgery? Which hospital? Which medicine? The child was home for only six weeks. Then she spent the rest of her life in a hospital, until she died at the age of three months.

But this year the world is filled with beauty and hope. Pessy called while holding her son in her arms. Pessy is busy all night and all day. She is now busy with normal things. "I'm too blessed to be stressed," she chuckled. I heard him gurgling as she spoke to me over the phone. It was a beautiful sound.

TRY

Try thinking about how beautiful something in your life would be if you did not take it for granted.

IN THE MERIT OF A BERACHAH

A *berachah* is a very precious thing. It is difficult for us to remember this for several reasons. *Berachos* are a part of our lifestyle and we begin saying them automatically. A thought that trips us up is that we think — what's the difference how I say this *berachah*? An action that is repeated many times daily doesn't have much impact, or does it?

Rav Chaim Shereshevsky *zt"l* taught us *Chumash* in High School. He was at least in his 70s at the time. My only wish is that we had paid closer attention to him. We didn't realize that this person in the rumpled suit with the European accent was actually a great *talmid chacham* who knew all of the Talmud by heart. Now when I look back at some of the *divrei Torah* he taught us I'm amazed at their practical and deep wisdom. I quoted him in my high school graduation speech and in many of my lectures.

Rav Shereshevsky taught us this *vort* (a Torah explanation that is short and to the point). When Eliezer came to the house of Besuel and Lavan to find a wife for Yitzchak, his hosts prepared a lavish meal for him. They also intended for it to be his last meal. His portion was poisoned. Eliezer said, "I am Avraham's servant, I cannot eat until I have said my words." The fundamental meaning is that Eliezer wanted to take care of his mission and to speak with Lavan and Besuel about Rivkah as a mate for Yitzchak. Rabbi Shereshevsky added, "Eliezer said, 'I will not eat until I say my words.' First Eliezer wanted to pray to Hashem. After that he had to wash and say a blessing, followed by a second blessing on the bread. During that time an angel came and switched the plates. Besuel died that night of food poisoning. Eliezer was not harmed." Rabbi Sheshevsky concluded, "The *baalei mussar* promise that if we are careful with our *berachos* we will not be harmed by the food we eat."

TRY

Try remembering how precious *berachos* are. When you recite a *berachah* think about its meaning.

OPPORTUNITY

Mornings are an opportunity to make the day joyous. When the sun rises we can become the sun shining on our household — we just have to make the decision. Although we may feel tired and our back might hurt, a smile will give us energy and moving around will ease the pain.

Instead of grumbling, shouting, or rushing around angrily, why not put our energy into being happy? Look around you and resolve that there are nice things to look at. Stop and listen to the young cheerful voices and decide you enjoy the song of a household beginning its day. Smell the coffee — literally. Savor the toast and add some jam to give your day a sweet beginning.

Don't let minor upsets chase your joy away. A soft calm heart will get things done just as quickly. Your morning is crucial. It sets the tone for your entire day.

TRY

One morning this week try thinking about the morning blessings (בִּרְכוֹת הַשַּׁחַר). When you open your eyes, think about and thank Hashem for the gift of vision. Then consider how much you have to thank Hashem for providing all your needs. It just might change your day.

DEAR REBBETZIN

Dear Rebbetzin,

I have lived in the neighborhood for seven years. It's been seven years of *Shabbosos* and *Yomim Tovim* that we have shared in *shul.* I want you to know that I have noticed in many ways your friendship, your ability to cheer people up, and your talent for recognizing the good in each person.

A smile! It seems so simple. You have a smile for everyone. I know that if guests come to my house from out of town and they come to your *shul* they will remember it fondly. I know that I can count on you for more than a smile and a friendly greeting. You will take the time to ask about my guests and to become interested in what they do, where they live, how they feel and what they need.

We are 100 people *davening* in *shul,* yet, each of us feels she is your personal friend. You always say, "It's so good to see you!" and you mean it!

I learned from you that it's possible to be friendly and warm to people you don't know very well. I have observed how you bring out the special qualities and talents of so many people in our *shul.*

I just wanted to let you know that every day you are making a difference in many lives.

TRY
Why not write a letter to your favorite Rebbetzin?

UNCERTAINTY

There are three things I can say about uncertainty: I struggle with it and want it to disappear. I know it will always be an issue until *Mashiach* comes. Everyone has to deal with it.

I struggle with it. I want insurance: medical insurance, life insurance, fire insurance, confidence and success insurance. A part of me wants to be finished when I've just begun. I want my project to be sold and delivered — finished, complete, and perfect. A part of me wants it *today*.

I want to know that my children are all happily married and their children already have their *shidduchim*. I want to know that we will always have health, sustenance and *nachas*. I want to be sure that my parents and mother-in-law will be fine. I want everyone who doesn't have a job to have one that they like.

However, there will always be uncertainty until *Mashiach* comes. There will always be a "what if." After all, we are only human. This is part of the way Hashem has set up the world. We walk in the fog of uncertainty and doubt and only Hashem knows anything indisputably. The only necessary insurance is trust and faith. Hashem is our source of confidence and hope.

Everyone, everyone, everyone has doubt. Doubt is a normal part of life. Rabbi Bachya Ibn Pekudah said that he didn't want to write his *sefer Chovos HaLevavos*. He was plagued with doubt as to its outcome — someone else could surely do it better. But he undertook the task despite his doubts. That's what all of us have to do. Simply close your eyes and jump in, not just once, but every day. Over and over again you have to say to that voice of doubt: I trust in Hashem. You just keep going forward and doing what you have to do. Persevere, for an hour, for 20 minutes, forever. From the moment you wake up until you go to sleep you must trust Hashem with the future and make the most of your present. When you feel yourself beset with doubt turn it into a prayer. And even in the prayer there is a doubt — "Do I know for certain that it was the right thing for me?" So you add a prayer for that doubt — Hashem You do what is best and in the best way.

We yearn for certainty, yet we know that only by learning to live with uncertainty and place our trust in G–d can we find peace of mind. We long to have all our doubts resolved, but life is uncertain and we aren't always in control. But when the world seems to be spinning out of control we must remember that SOMEONE is driving and steering us in the right direction.

TRY

Before you go to sleep try thinking about the last words of *Adon Olam* —
"Hashem is with me, I will not fear."

HANDSHAKE

The lecture took place 20 years ago, yet I remember much of it precisely. I remember Rebbetzin Grunfeld's *o"h* dignity and her imposing demeanor. She stood in a long black dress. Her jacket looked like a cape. Her black wig had an intricate pearl netting in the back. Her words were poetic and her voice had a melodious tone. The lecture was punctuated with gestures, laughter and emotion. Everyone in the audience felt a combination of kinship and awe.

With her words she transported us to the Polish countryside. WE met Sarah Schenirer together with her and saw those first Bais Yaakov students studying Torah under the trees. After the lecture I went up to say thank you. She took my hand in both of hers and held it. The Rebbetzin looked directly into my eyes as I spoke. I felt that I had her complete attention. She continued holding my hand. The Rebbetzin asked, "What is your name?" I stammered. I hadn't expected her to ask. "Your name is important to me," she said. "I want to remember you." I'm certain I'll always remember her handshake.

I'm often asked to address a large audience. It's always a privilege and a pleasure. Sometimes there are 100 people in the audience and sometimes 1,000. After the lecture a few people will come up and say thank you or ask a question. When I speak with them I think of Rebbetzin Grunfeld. When I shake hands I try to connect with the person I'm meeting. It's just a few moments, but can I make them last?

TRY

Try giving your undivided attention to whomever you speak to. It truly makes the individual feel better.

THE POWER OF SMALL ACTIONS

Your unique magnificent ideal can only be activated through many small actions — some are public while others are performed privately. Don't just sit there and dream unhappily — do something! You might think that it doesn't pay to try because no one will notice your efforts. However, if you persist, your time will come. The heartwarming incident that follows reassured me that the possibilities are beyond our imagination.

> Tens of thousands arrived in Lublin. They came to celebrate the laying of the cornerstone for Yeshivas Chachmei Lublin. The Yeshivah was built on a plot that Reb Shmuel Eichenbaum had donated. Rav Yisrael of Tchortkov was standing near Reb Shmuel. Rav Yisrael said, "I do not envy you sir, that you gave the plot for the yeshivah and are the guest of honor today. After all, this is a public *mitzvah* and it brings with it feelings of conceit. I envy you sir, for the *mitzvah* you did in secret previously, the one through which you merited this one" (*MiMayenos HaNezach*, p. 205).

The incident in *Tanach* about Devorah *HaNeviah* teaches us how "an ordinary woman" who quietly did her best to serve Hashem became a leader of the Jewish nation.

> "And Devorah was a prophetess, the wife of Lapidos. She judged the nation of Israel at that time." *Tanna d'Vei Eliyahu* says, "Who was Devorah? Who was this renowned woman who judged the Jewish nation and said prophecy? After all, Pinchas the son of Elazar was also a leader at that time. I call heaven and earth to stand witness to the truth of my statement. Whether man or woman, servant or maidservant, what happens to you depends only on your actions. Everyone can earn the privilege of the spirit of Heavenly insight being with him."
>
> Devorah's husband was unlearned. His wife said, "I have an idea. I will make wicks for you and you will bring

them to the House of Hashem in Shiloh. Perhaps thereby your portion will be with the righteous and you will have a share in the World to Come." Devorah prepared thick wicks so that their light would be increasingly bright; therefore he was called *Lapidos* (a flame).

Hashem knows a person's thoughts and intent. Hashem said to Devorah, "You intended to glorify My Name and you made thick wicks so that their light would be very bright. I will increase your influence in Israel, Judah and the ten tribes" (from *Yalkut Shimoni*).

Devorah made wicks to beautify the House of Hashem in Shiloh. This is an act with which we can identify. Many of us are creative with our hands. Yet she was not tempted to let ordinary wicks suffice. Her wicks were thick. The *Metzudas David* says that she worked with enthusiasm and did her absolute best. Her reward was very great, as the *Ralbag* explains, "The word *Lapidos* can be an adjective describing Devorah." The *Ralbag* continues, "When she spoke one saw flames surrounding her, as the Torah describes in reference to Moshe *Rabbeinu*. She was already at that magnificent level of prophecy. She inspired the Jews to return wholeheartedly to Hashem."

I thought about this. Do we know for how long Devorah made these wicks? Do we know the extent of her wholehearted faith? We do know that she didn't give up and she didn't seek honor. However, Hashem saw her actions and she was rewarded with increased opportunities for closeness to Hashem. Hashem chose her to lead the Jewish nation.

Our deeds every day; our routine actions; the way we speak; the way we listen; the way we do our daily work — *these* are what Hashem is looking at. They are what is truly important. The story of Elkanah illustrates this concept:

Elkanah was a prophet. He was the father of Shmuel the prophet who is described by King David as equal to Moshe and Aharon. The sages describe his ascent to leadership: "First he advanced in his home. People admired his private life and began following his advice in his neighborhood. After that his influence rose in the city. Hashem saw his noble spirit and made his name known in all the land of Israel. Nevertheless, his rise in influence was because of his essential qualities. As the *Zayis Raanan* explains, "It was not because of wealth and not because of lineage but because of his great deeds."

Don't be discouraged. If you want to get ahead you will find the way. Don't be deterred by the obstacles you face. Just begin today to do what you know is right. Hashem sees. Hashem hears. Your time will come.

TRY

Try making some wicks ... What does the symbol of the "wicks" mean to you?

AN IMPORTANT VISITOR

I woke up early that morning and I was at the store by 8:30. I stopped at the bakery aisle and bought Kaiser rolls, danishes and bread. Then I went to the dairy case and bought the home-made vegetable cream cheese and some lox. I took a new jar of coffee. I thought of my guest as I shopped. I hope she'll be happy at our home. She's so famous, an influential lawyer in Chicago.

The doorbell rang. Everyone looked up. My eleven-year-old son went to the door. I imagined that he was welcoming the prime minister, not a distant relative of ours. I drew a deep breath. My kids like to play, run around and sometimes have loud arguments. I really wanted them to be well-behaved and polite to my guest, but I didn't know if saying something would help or hurt the situation.

"Please be good," I thought. "Please help me that it should work out," I prayed. Sholom was speaking slowly and carefully, "It's such a pleasure to see you. May I take your bag and show you to your room." I smiled. A butler couldn't have done it better. A few minutes later I heard him again, "Would you, perhaps, like to have some tea and cake?"

I had been busy preparing for our company all afternoon. I enjoyed perfecting every minute detail. The house smelled like a grassy meadow. Everything sparkled. I was just about to put my *challah* loaves into the oven when our cousin joined me in the kitchen. My oldest daughter brought tea cups and plates to the table. She took a lovely platter of cake out of the fridge.

Our cousin wore a black dress and a matching pill-box hat. She smiled as she glanced at my five children. They took the cue and introduced themselves. They sat politely around the table, smiling and answering her questions in polite voices. Everyone was saying "please," speaking softly and saying "thank you." Instead of reaching over, they remembered to ask a sibling to pass the sugar.

Tonight we would all be attending a family wedding. Each child was excited about wearing her favorite dress and shiny black shoes. After a while my daughters went upstairs to get ready. They spoke quietly even upstairs and the older children helped their younger sister get dressed. My eldest curled her sister's hair in a flip and even let her use her favorite bow — the one that she has always kept on the right hand side of the dresser drawer for the last three years.

It was time to take out the *challah*, and this week it was high and brown. My cousin watched, "Do you bake *challah* every week?" "I began about five years ago," I said with a smile.

The bell rang and my husband was at the door. "I'll go up and get ready for the wedding," he said. I smiled to my guest and excused myself too. My children were all at the top-floor landing when I came up.

I hugged them all. "Thank you children. Thank you for sharing with each other and for caring for our guest. I was worried, but now I'm proud. You behaved magnificently. You've made our guest happy."

As I dressed for the wedding I smiled and reflected. True, my cousin's position was impressive, her power and renown were legendary. I stayed home and baked, cooked, and cared for my children. Yet when my children behaved as they did tonight and understood what to do without my explanations it made me feel splendidly regal.

TRY

Try looking at your family and remembering that each child is amazing. Try to validate and nurture each person. Help each child accept himself a little better. If you can do this your family will become closer.

WHERE DID THE YEARS GO?

We sat in long rows in our eighth-grade classroom, a sea of navy blue jumpers. Every Monday morning our teacher wrote a saying on the blackboard and we memorized it during the week. This week it was a long saying and it took her a few minutes to write it all down. She turned and said, "This saying is very meaningful to me. It is to your benefit to try to comprehend its meaning before it is too late."

> Man worries about losing his money.
> Man doesn't worry about losing his days.
> His days do not return,
> His money does not help.

We took out our notebooks and wrote down the saying and we couldn't understand why our teacher thought this saying was so vital. When you are 13 you feel that you and everyone you know will live forever.

The years passed and I remembered this saying. I hate to count all the years that I remembered this saying. Ironically it has given me a sense of purpose and comfort. In wise perspective there is comfort.

Everyone has problems. Everyone has losses, great and small. Our dreams and plans can shatter. An object can break. At those times a healthy perspective helps and I remember this saying. We worry about losing money and because of that our days are wasted. In the end, even if we have the money our days will never return. So, let go of the loss and enjoy the day.

There are people we all know who never took the time to enjoy life. They didn't play with a child. They didn't take a walk in the sunshine or go to a park. They rarely sat and listened to someone they loved. There was always more and more work to be done. There were a few more dollars to be earned. Then they grow old and they have the money but the days are lost. Theirs was a life full of tension, stress and hurt feelings. One can try to buy back lost time with money but it never works. The money never compensates. The money cannot fill the hole in the soul.

Ultimately our time is our most precious resource. Today is yours. Whatever you hope to do, try to do it today. Decide to do everything with happiness and determination. Decide to improve your world today. You may not be 13, but it isn't too late.

TRY

Try to remind yourself from time to time — THIS IS IT! Try to always remember to value the proper things in life. Make every day count!

GOOD FEELINGS INVENTORY

When can I sit down and think about the good feelings I am experiencing? Perhaps Friday night is an opportune time. After I light the candles I can sit and reflect on the good things that are happening in my life right now. I can think about the past week and gather those pearls of good feelings that I hadn't stopped to notice all week.

I can think about the proud feeling. The proud feeling came when my son picked out a document frame and said, "Mommy, can we get this?" As soon as we arrived home he rushed to get his award for learning 1,000 *mishnayos* and lovingly placed it in the frame. "Where can I hang this, Mommy?" he asked. I hesitated for just a second and then said, "In the dining room."

I can stop to savor laughter and joy. I look at little Rochel, only 10-months-old, yet she has so much to be happy about. She claps her little hands and laughs merrily. It takes so little to make her happy — a smile, a quick game of peek-a-boo, or when she stands on her own two feet. All of these make her smile and laugh.

I can caress the feeling of peace, the warm soft glow of candlelight. There is nowhere to rush away to. Right now there is the peace of Shabbos and the calmness of knowing Hashem is here in our home with us.

I can feel confident as I ponder small accomplishments. This week I found the jacket that was missing for three months. This week I prepared fresh chicken soup instead of using some from the freezer. This week I tried a new recipe and it came out good. This week we stayed on a salt-free diet and we all feel healthier.

I can feel hopeful about my efforts. I can hope that my dream of completing the course and becoming a certified homeopath will occur sometime in the future. I can hope that my writing will appear in a book. I can hope that my children will be happy and have friends this summer.

Rabbi Salanter says that negative feelings come of themselves, but good feelings take conscious effort. We will all gain if we make time to gather the good feelings on a regular basis.

TRY

After you light the Shabbos candles try to sit down and think about the good things that are happening in your life right now.

BOWING BEFORE HASHEM

Rabbi Avigdor Miller discusses two elements in bowing before Hashem and urges us to utilize both of them.

It is fundamentally important for a man to realize that he is nothing at all. What are we? Like a dream that goes away. The *neshamah,* however, is extremely important. It's a part of G-d breathed into man. However, no one becomes arrogant because of the *neshamah.* All human pride is based on physical things — whether looks, height, strength, money or power. Alone you are nothing and you cannot do a thing to help yourself. We are like a piece of clay in the Creator's hands. Therefore one of the purposes of bowing down is to bring yourself low before Hashem.

It's a great asset. Our great men were chosen only because they had this character trait. Hashem chooses the humble ones. Moshe *Rabbeinu* was the most humble of men.

Why did Hashem show Moshe the knot of His *tefillin* and all the secrets of the Torah? It was because of his humility.

Humility will help you to succeed in life. People who are leaders must at least try to show humility. If one complains to the bank or company president he must listen politely.

When you bow down it pays to utilize the opportunity to acquire humility. Think to yourself, "I am lowering myself before Hashem and everything is in Hashem's hands."

The second element in bowing is to remember Hashem's awesome majesty. Realize the greatness of the King of the Universe — Hashem rules the entire universe. Be aware that there is no searching out G-d's greatness. Therefore when you bow down think for a moment how Hashem rules the entire universe.

What are some details of Hashem's majesty that we can contemplate? Rav Levi Yitzchak of Berditchev says, "Think about the Creator and the armies of angels serving Him. Each angel is flawless, pure, energetic, and can traverse the entire universe in seconds. Yet these angels are insignificant when they are compared to the higher angels called *Ofanim* and *Chayos.* All the angels together anxiously await the opportunity to praise Hashem and they utter His praises with great awe and fear."

What feelings do these thoughts generate? Rav Levi Yitzchak continues, "When we contemplate these details we are filled with awe, yet simultaneously with great joy. Although Hashem is a Great King, our words of Torah and *tefillah* are very precious to Him. Hashem established the world so that all the bounty in the higher and lower spheres depends on the actions of man."

Therefore when one bows before Hashem with the proper intent he is drawing down blessing from the higher worlds to our world. We bend our knees as we say, "*Baruch*" and thereby become a vessel to receive Hashem's gifts.

Rav Levi Yitzchak then explains that our sages have revealed to us an even higher level than this when they told us to straighten up as we say Hashem's Name. When we straighten up we are giving something to Hashem. "We have brought Hashem *nachas* with our prayer, because our prayer has caused Hashem's Name to be sanctified and to become great in all the worlds" (*Kedushas Levi, Lech Lecha*).

Here is a list that summarizes the main points that we can think of when we bow down before Hashem during our prayers.

HUMILITY	On our own we are nothing.
MAJESTY OF THE CREATOR	(a) Hashem rules the entire universe. (b) The perfect angels praise Hashem.
JOY	Our words of Torah and *tefillah* are precious to Hashem.
REWARD	We draw down Hashem's bounty to our world.
A GIFT	We have brought Hashem *nachas* with our prayers.

PURIM SNAPSHOTS

I look at the Purim pictures that we took several years ago. My nine-year-old daughter Chavy was a fancy lady on Purim. She wore my old fur jacket. Chaya Rivky was a Queen. Shulim was a very cute cowboy. He had a costume with fringes, a red bandanna, a cowboy hat and of course a gun in a holster. Aaron was a very kissable *sefer Torah*. We made the costume out of blue velour and painted a crown and *luchos* on the front with fabric paint. My niece made the front of the costume for me.

Purim — we strive to add new meaning to a joyous and important day. What can we do to make this day extraordinary? How can we share our joy even more? How can we feel Hashem's presence and remember the miracles of that time?

I'd like to share with all of you some Purim "snapshots." Some of these are actual pictures I've seen and some are word pictures — short anecdotes from past Purims that have made my Purim holiday more meaningful.

AN OPEN HOUSE

My former landlady is called "Nenie" by everyone. Nenie means aunt in Hungarian and she is everyone's aunt. She has an open house. Everyone can come and visit. Nenie looks forward to surprises and means it when she says, "I'm so happy to see you."

After Purim, Nenie showed me a picture her nephew had taken at 1 a.m. on Purim morning. Nenie is in the center of the photo. Her face is brilliant with a radiant smile. Towering around her are seven 15-year-old boys dressed like soldiers.

Nenie explained, "Well, my nephews are learning in the yeshivah in South Fallsburg, but they all wanted to be in Boro Park for Purim, and they needed a place to stay. I opened my home to them. They left their *mishloach manos* here between deliveries. They stopped in during the day for a snack and then later came to the Purim meal, and finally at 1 a.m. they came back to sleep for the night. They were so happy that they had successfully collected money for *tzedakah*. They said they must take a picture with me. Then I made them all a place to sleep on the living room floor."

I looked at the picture and I thought, do I know anyone who needs a "home base" in the neighborhood? Is there someone who needs a place to perhaps hear the *Megillah*, leave their *mishloach manos*, come for the *seudah* and sleep over? We can all learn from Nenie how to joyously perform the *mitzvah* of *hachnasas orchim*.

REMEMBERING YOUR NEIGHBORS

About two decades ago I was shown a picture in camp by my friend. It showed her mother's dining-room table covered with hundreds of tiny *mishloach manos*. "We live in Long Beach," Batya explained. "There are many elderly people in the community who live alone and their families are far away. My mother gives out about 200 *mishloach manos* to these neighbors. For some it's the only *mishloach manos* they will receive on Purim."

When I was a *kallah* I prepared about 50 *mishloach manos* and distributed them in the Old Age Home on Foster Avenue.

Most of us don't know what to do with all the candy we receive on Purim, but what about those people whom no one remembers? What about those who sit alone all day on Purim and their homes are quiet, too quiet?

It took my husband Feivy two hours to deliver the Boro Park *mishloach manos* and another one and a half hours to deliver in Flatbush. That is when we made a shorter list. I now send a card and a donation for *tzedakah* instead of *mishloach manos* to friends who I know receive dozens of packages anyway. However, I still have my private list and every year I hire a messenger to deliver the most important *mishloach manos* on my list. These *mishloach manos* are significant because perhaps they are the only ones that particular person will receive on Purim.

TIME FOR YOUR OWN ELDERLY RELATIVES

It was the day before Purim. I was looking over the *mishloach manos* and checking my lists to be sure that all the little details were under control. I jumped up and ran to get the costume that still needed to be hemmed. The phone rang.

It was my niece. We started discussing our Purim plans. Suddenly my niece said, "I was thinking about Purim when I was very young. There were all these relatives we used to visit who were from the past generation. Each year they were fewer and fewer. Now I can't think of anyone from that generation who is left. Those few people represented a world that is disappearing."

I tried to find a comforting perspective on this. "After all," I said, "most of these people would be in their high 90s if they were alive today. We were fortunate for the times we were there to visit, to listen and to learn."

"Certainly," my niece replied. "But isn't it funny, when we were younger and busier we were sure these relatives would just be there forever. Of course I always went on Purim, but there were so many other times when I could have visited and didn't because I was busy with trivialities."

My grandmother felt that whenever possible you should give of yourself completely and do your best for others. She treated every person, even young children, with respect and warmth. I loved talking to her because she would stop everything to hold my hand, look in my eyes and listen carefully to what I was saying. Her satisfaction stemmed from giving and therefore she was always happy.

On Purim, Bubby was the queen of giving. She presided over a table overflowing with 100 *mishloach manos* plates. Every friend, relative, neighbor and acquaintance stopped by. Everyone received a plate of her homemade cookies, rumballs, and other treats — all beautifully wrapped. She knew what each person who visited was most interested in and made them feel welcome. I wonder now how she did it all!

FRIENDSHIPS AND THANK YOU

Two smiling friends wearing funny hats. They are holding champagne glasses in the air, filled with ginger ale. *L'Chaim* and Happy Purim!

If you feel too shy to visit someone but you want to renew a friendship, Purim is a good time to stop in and wish them well. If you used to keep in touch but haven't called in months, Purim is a good day to say "Hello." Purim can be a "thank you" day. Thank you to the mother who does car-pool and the neighbor who helps you in myriads of ways. Thank you to the person who keeps your spare key in case you get locked out ... What a great opportunity to show your appreciation!

WHO WILL GIVE FIRST?

It's a mistake to think that success depends on whether or not others approve of you. You cannot change or control anyone but yourself. My daughter was discussing Purim with me. "I'm going to bring a *mishloach manos* basket to school so that in case someone thinks of giving me one I'll be ready with one to give back."

We decided she would just give *mishloach manos* to whomever she wanted to be friendly with and not wait for the other person to give first. Hopefully this girl will reciprocate and if she doesn't then Chavi has acted in the true spirit of Purim.

My daughter's struggle happens so often in our lives. So many times people wait for others to think of them first. One can spend a lifetime waiting!

Our sages teach us that the key to true success is to consider others first and show you care about them.

On Purim I brought hamentashen to an older woman who I knew wouldn't have made them for herself. You can also offer *latkes* on Chanukah.

On Purim the *mitzvah* is to give *tzedakah* to everyone who asks. We all strive to have an open hand. Hashem says, "My hand is open too, to grant your requests."

ABSENTMINDED

I had an original theory about absentmindedness and efficiency when I was in the third grade. It had to do with folders. Chanie, who sat in the desk on my left, had perfect folders in five colors. When our teacher asked for a sheet, she pulled out a starched, white, never-wrinkled stencil from the appropriate folder, in one second. Her pencil case contained sharpened pencils and pink erasers. Since Chanie never made a mistake the eraser was there just for fun. Her books were neatly stacked. Her notebooks had labels. I knew why Chanie's briefcase was so perfect. Chanie's mother was super-organized.

I saw miracles every day. At ten o'clock the teacher would ask for the *Chumash* homework. My hand would go to my mouth. Where is my homework? I worked on it for half an hour last night, but then I left it on the dining-room table. I could see it now, near the empty orange juice container. I checked my briefcase because that was what everyone else was doing. However, I knew that the situation was pretty hopeless. I put my hand in my grammar folder and pulled out my *Chumash* sheet. Wow! It's a miracle. I thanked Hashem and promised to be more careful next time.

Now I am a mother. My third grader spends an hour preparing her things every night. She empties her briefcase and files away her sheets in color-coded folders. She sharpens all her pencils to perfect points. She goes through a pack of pencils each week because she sharpens pencils endlessly. She prepares her lunch and lays out her clothes. I watch her and suddenly I realize, "It wasn't Chanie's mother after all, it was Chanie who was super-organized!"

After the children are asleep I straighten up the dining room and kitchen. I notice my fourth grader's homework near the coke bottle. I pick up the sheet, open her briefcase and slip it into a folder. I realize with a smile that tomorrow someone will experience a miracle.

TRY

Sometimes it's only when we are in the same situation that we realize the numerous small things our mothers did to make our lives pleasant. It's never too late to say "thank you."

A LESSON IN TEHILLIM

MIZMOR SHIR CHANUKAS HABAYIS LEDAVID

The thirtieth psalm in *Tehillim* was said at many important beginnings. It was sung on the day that the *Bais HaMikdash* was dedicated. Each year when millions of Jews marched up to Jerusalem bearing baskets of *bikkurim* (first fruits) they were greeted by the Levites with this psalm. It was sung when the *Bais HaMikdash* was rededicated by the *Chashmonaim* on Chanukah. Today, many people inaugurate the daily prayers with this psalm and say it each night when the Chanukah lights are burning.

The first thought David expresses is, אֲרוֹמִמְךָ ה' כִּי דִלִּיתָנִי וְלֹא שִׂמַּחְתָּ אֹיְבַי לִי, "I will raise You up Hashem because You have pulled me up [from the depths] and You did not let my enemy rejoice over me" (30:2).

Rav Shamshon Raphael Hirsch notes that the word דִלִּיתָנִי appears in this form only here, and he explains the concept at great length. דִלִּיתָנִי is from the root דְּלִי — a pail. Hashem drew David up out of danger as a pail is pulled out of the well. What supports the pail? It is only the rope that holds it from ABOVE. If the rope breaks the pail will fall and be lost in the deep well. David declares that his protection and his sole mainstay is Hashem Above.

It's something to pause and think about. How strong is the "rope" that connects us to Hashem right now? From what is this rope formed? How can we strengthen our ties to the ABOVE?

When things are difficult, the dark narrow confines of sadness and discouragement are very painful. Our normal resources and intuition seem more limited than usual. We can't escape dwelling on the negative and we can't imagine a way out of the present predicament.

In the sixth verse David *HaMelech* tells us why we should not become discouraged when facing adversity, — כִּי רֶגַע בְּאַפּוֹ חַיִּים בִּרְצוֹנוֹ בָּעֶרֶב יָלִין בֶּכִי וְלַבֹּקֶר רִנָּה, "For His anger lasts but a moment; life results from His favor. In the evening one lies down weeping, but with the dawn there will be a cry of joy."

First David *HaMelech* says that G-d's anger lasts for a moment. Although we feel hopelessly sunk in despair now, the adversity will pass. David also says that Hashem's intention is always to set us on the road to a happy life. You may not know how a good future can possibly come out of the bleak present, but Hashem is planning to bestow great gifts upon you. Finally, the *pasuk* says that the night in our lives isn't all black; there will be a dawn. Your life will contain many times of joyous song.

It might help to think of some time in the past when you were ill, or in danger, or in pain, or worried about something major. How did Hashem help you then? How was the problem resolved? I think that everyone over age 25 has experienced at least one miracle in their life, if not many. Just as Hashem helped in the past there will be a dawn — a time of joy — again.

In a little town in Austria, not far from the Russian border, there lived two people: Moshe, a Jew, and Johannes, his non- Jewish neighbor. Both were working people, and they got along well. Then times turned bad and they were both forced to go out into the street and beg for alms. When Pesach approached Johannes began to wonder what he would do during the holidays.

"I have an idea," said Moshe. "I'll get you a hat and coat like mine, and I'll take you along with me to the synagogue. People will think you're Jewish. You'll get invited to a *Seder* and your problems about food will be over."

Johannes waited at the *Seder* table, impatient for the moment when the meal would begin. The host began with *Kiddush*, then everyone washed their hands. But instead of a meal everyone was given a small piece of onion, which they dipped into salt water before eating. He then saw the host take out a matzah and break it in two, but instead of eating some of it, the host just took the bigger piece and hid it away! Then the host began to recite the *Haggadah*. They continued to read from the holy book for what seemed like hours, while Johannes tried to turn the pages at their pace. Finally the host washed again. Now Johannes was hopeful that the meal would be served.

Before eating his small piece of matzah, Johannes watched to be sure that this time his host was actually eating the matzah as well. After that, much to Johannes' chagrin, the host took a sizable portion of ground horseradish for himself, and then handed a like portion to his guest. Johannes tried his best to eat the horseradish. His eyes were tearing and his whole body arched forward as he tried to swallow the bitter herbs. He had hardly finished eating this first portion when he saw his host prepare another portion of horseradish for everyone, only this time with matzah.

His anger raged, he got up, threw the matzah with the horseradish on the table, and ran to the door, yelling: "You can all keep your Pesach with its bitterness!"

Moshe arrived home a few hours later, happy and satisfied from a wonderful Pesach repast and saw Johannes lying in bed. Johannes immediately began grumbling about the terrible night he had at the *Seder.*

"If only you would have waited one more minute you would have been served fish, soup, meat, side dishes, and dessert. You admit that there was good food prepared. Surely the family intended to eat a regular meal as soon as they finished the customary deeds that every Jew practices at the *Seder.* It was only a question of one minute more."

"This," concluded the Kotzker Rebbe, "is a lesson of faith. A Jew must always have the faith and patience to be able to tolerate that last moment!" (*And Nothing But The Truth,* pp. 79-85).

For His anger lasts but a moment; life results from His favor. In the evening one lies down weeping, but with the dawn, there will be a shout of joy!

CHINESE AUCTION

I entered the yeshivah membership tea, along with a close friend and neighbor. Dee stood before me on line and bought 15 raffle tickets. She turned to me with a smile and said, "Here are seven for you." I was so surprised, I didn't know what to say other than, "Thank you." Then I stepped up and bought some tickets. I handed five to her and said, "I had already promised the money for the yeshivah so I bought a lot of tickets. I wonder if the tickets you bought for me will be lucky ones?" I chuckled. "I hope you win something tonight, Dee. I never win at these things, but it's the *mitzvah* that counts."

Today, for the first time in my life I won an enjoyable prize. The last time I won a raffle prize it consisted of a tie my husband would never wear and a polo shirt in an outrageous color. However, this time I won a prize I needed. Yesterday I said to my daughter, "Wouldn't it be nice to have a good-quality photo album? Pictures are treasures and everlasting memories and if I could save them in a nice place they'd last longer. They wouldn't get lost or torn."

I walked out the next morning and Dee's son was at my corner. He handed me a package. "You won this from my yeshivah," he said. He smiled as he explained, "My mother won something too."

I opened up my box and found a leather-bound Holson photo album. It's about 11" by 17" and bound in black leather. It's the kind you see in the photo store but leave on the shelf when you look at the price. I spent an hour this afternoon sorting pictures and remembering the past year and its moments of joy. I put a special label on each page and slipped my favorite photos into the pockets. What perfect timing, I thought. Just this week my husband brought home about 150 photographs from the photo store.

I smiled when I saw the picture we took at the picnic with my cousins. Then I saw the picture of my son standing and smiling proudly with his certificate — "best student of the month." I felt excited again for my son whose team had won color war, as I looked at his picture with his team's banner. The banner was his idea. On the next page I slipped in the wedding pictures of my first cousin. Pictures are fun.

I feel that this luxury came as a blessing from Hashem. Dee, I think your friendly gesture really made a difference. When I enjoy the album I'll remember your present of raffle tickets and your thoughtfulness. I hope you are always a winner.

TRY

We often have opportunities to enhance a relationship through a simple but thoughtful gesture. To whom can you be a friend today?

EXTRA LARGE

When you were born you there was an extra large celebration in the heavens and on earth. Your parents looked at you and said, "*Baruch Hashem.*" You were tiny, but their joy was extra large. They looked at you, with your red wrinkled face and no hair and said, "She's so beautiful. She's a miracle. She's a gift from Hashem." They were relaxed and ecstatic that the wait was over, and now everything would be fine.

When you were born your parents had extra large dreams for you. "We want to make this child happy. We are wiser now and we want to use that wisdom well. We want to give her all the joy we couldn't give to the others. We don't want to spoil her, however. May Hashem help us to raise a *mentch.*"

Those first ten minutes of your life were extra large. They were full of breathtaking emotion and deeply felt sentiment. Those moments were fresh and beautiful. Your parents smiled, and cried and gently caressed you. They held you and gazed at you with a wondering look in their eyes. The beginning of new life rekindles our deepest resources.

Those extra large moments when you were extra small are usually kept secret. People generally can't find the words to talk about the extra large moments of life. However, if you pause to reflect — you can know all about it even without words.

TRY

Tomorrow morning keep this thought of Rabbi Shlomo Ganzfried, *zt"l*, in mind: "Every morning we are created anew."

Ph.D. IN PARENTING

by Cipora Shazuri Weber

After many years of waiting I have received my Ph.D. I am now a professional stay-at-home mother. I cook and bake — even after I have stayed awake through the night caring for my child's bronchitis. I have become a whiz at wiping runny noses and pointing out blossoming roses. After repeatedly tying open shoelaces I am greeted with my children's warm smiling faces. I hand them a snack and give them a hug or a pat on their back.

When the corporate giants ask me, "What do you do for a living?" I answer, "I provide a kitchen that's healthy and nourishing."

"Oh! Do you work in a soup kitchen for the homeless?" they ask.

I smile as I confess that I make sure that my family is in a home it can bless!

> # TRY:
>
> **Mothers are constantly doing something for someone. Let's think of reasons why we like to.**

[Cipora Shazuri Weber is the creator of "Life Lessons" workshops which include "forgiveness" and "happiness." She also does individual counseling.]

A BERACHAH LEVATALAH (in vain)
by David Zaritsky

This incident illustrates the power of *berachos* over the food we eat.

When the German Nazis, *yemach shemam,* entered this particular village they gathered the wealthy Jews and locked them up in order to force them to sign over their possessions. They were imprisoned without food. Finally, after many hours, the Germans gave them salty food to eat and they became desperately thirsty. The Germans promised a drink and freedom to anyone who would sign over his property. As each individual surrendered and signed, they forced him to pass through the room alone. Presumably he was served a drink and set free.

Our story's main character went into the room and reached for a drink. At the last second he stopped himself. He had always been a believing Jew and even at this desperate moment he would not forget to recite the *berachah,* "*shehakol nihiyeh bidvaro.*" As he pronounced the words he noticed the German laughing at him. His hand that held the glass began to shake. An overwhelming feeling gripped him. It only took a moment to throw the water on the floor.

He turned to the German and said, "I'm not going to drink this water. It's poisoned." The German pushed him out the door and told him to run and never return. He was the only survivor of that group.

This man had made a *berachah levatalah* — a *berachah* for nothing, because he had made a *berachah* but he didn't drink. However, the *berachah* saved his life!

TRY

Pause and reflect before you say a *berachah.* Pay close attention to the words. You will remain with more than you expected.

FRIDAY NIGHT
by Gitty Kar

From the time I was a small girl I remember my mother telling me that every Friday night a special *malach* (angel) comes to the window. If the table is set and the candles are lit and the house is peaceful, the *malach* says, "May next week be the same."

When I argued with my siblings and it was almost time to light the candles, my mother would say, "The *malach* is coming. Let's make peace so that the arguing and anxiety should not be wished upon us for next week also." We quickly stopped arguing and Friday night was peaceful. As soon as my mother put on her white kerchief and covered her eyes, the house was enveloped in calm and peace.

When I was married, my husband's grandmother presented me with a lace mantilla that she had made for me. I wear it when I *bench lecht*. From Shabbos *sheva berachos* on, as soon as I *bench lecht,* peace enters the house. It is impossible to describe it.

When I cover my eyes to light the candles and make the *berachos,* I make an effort to be dressed in honor of Shabbos. I don't even wear slippers. The Shabbos Queen comes to give us a Shabbos that is peaceful and rejuvenating. Shabbos gives us strength and energy for the whole week.

TRY

On Shabbos are lives are less hurried. Take the time to listen to your inner voice and to feel the calm of Shabbos on a deeper level.

TWENTY-FIVE WAYS TO TELL YOUR CHILD, "I LOVE YOU"

1) Come up with a new anagram for your child's initials. For instance, Chaya Rivkah Weinreich's initials might stand for **C**reative, **R**esponsible, **W**onderful.

2) Leave surprise messages in unexpected places — on the door of your child's closet, on cereal boxes, in your child's lunch box. Post-it notes work well for this.

3) Mail a letter or card to your child, even if they haven't gone away. When we went away and my children stayed with relatives for a few days, I packed a letter and a small prize for my children with instructions that they open up one package each day that we were away.

4) Decorate a placemat with a personalized message such as "Eating Spot of the Best Six-Year-Old in the Whole World."

5) Make your child a needlepoint picture or pillow. My grandmother prepared an elaborate needlepoint for my wedding present. She wrapped it up in tissue paper and put it in a drawer. Although my grandmother o"h was *niftar* when I was 14, the needlepoint she made for me is hanging in my living room. I remember her whenever I look at it.

6) If you are reading aloud from a picture book, change the name of the main character to that of your child.

7) Tell your child, "I'm so glad Hashem gave you to me!" One child told his mother, "I'm so glad Hashem picked you to be my mother."

8) At the end of the day, tell your child you appreciate all the good things he or she did that day, such as picking up toys and sharing a snack with a sibling.

9) Hang up a "Welcome Home" sign on the front door as a surprise, after the first day of school or any other day.

10) Occasionally allow your child to drink from your crystal goblet or serve him/ her supper on your good china. I fondly remember that whenever I visited my great-aunt Rivkah she always served me soda in her fanciest crystal glass. She said to me, "You are my company now. I trust you with the glass."

11) Frame an award your child received and hang it up in the dining room (or any other prominent place).

12) Plan a scavenger hunt with a map and a series of clues that leads to a prize or an I.O.U. for a special trip.

13) When you light Shabbos candles remind your children that each of them makes the world brighter.

14) Go for a special walk together with one child at a time. For a while I gave each child a turn to go for a short walk with me on Friday after school.

15) On a clear night, look at the stars together with your children. Remind them that although the stars appear small actually they are much bigger than the earth, and so it is with each of us.

16) Put some pictures of your children doing things they are proud of on your fridge. For example — I have a picture of my son with the intricate LEGO boat he put together.

17) Smile! Smile some more!

18) Tell your children when they've done a job well.

19) "Talk to each of your children at their eye level" (Rabbi Ezriel Tauber).

20) Play a board game together.

21) Write a long list with your child of all the things that he or she can do.

22) Tell your child three positive messages before they fall asleep and when they first wake up each morning.

23) Arrange for your child to visit someone who brings out the best in them.

24) If your child is worried about something, like a test, give some *tzedakah* and pray about it together. Never pressure them about things like grades if you know they are doing the best they can.

25) Sing *Hallel* together whenever you can.

The Last Word

I began W.H.A.T. CAN RELIEVE STRESS with a dedication to the past — to my grandparents. I beg for stories and facts. I feel a tug at my heart when I discover that some details can no longer be remembered. I feel that a life has been extinguished — one that I will never know.

Perhaps I know my ancestor's life better than I had first supposed. Much has changed but the fundamental components of our spiritual past lives on.

What town did you come from? Who were your ancestors? Everyone has an ancestor and everyone carries an inner spark. We carry a light from the past that we need to be conscious of constantly. Our ancestors live on in our prayers, *mitzvos*, and acts of kindness.

I'm concluding this book with a dedication to the future. W.H.A.T. CAN RELIEVE STRESS is a little book with big ideas. The suggestions you have read are different from those you will find in other books of this genre. These are Torah suggestions that are rooted in our illustrious past. I hope the Torah outlook you gain will inspire you and direct you in your search for tranquility.

Any single step opens the door. We can look directly at a child and tell them some encouraging WORDS. We can experiment with the HABIT of gratitude and experience serenity. We can decide on a course of ACTION by emulating a terrific person we know. We can share an inspiring THOUGHT or story. Why not consider that anything might be possible?

Thank you for reading my book. Now I hope you will use it. You are standing at the door to your future. Opportunities to celebrate life await you. Don't just read about the past, jump in and initiate your glowing future.

About the Author

Roiza Devorah Weinreich, best-selling author of *There Will Never Be Another You, In-Joy* and *A Happier You* (for teens), has designed and presented practical workshops based on Torah principles and true success stories for the past 13 years. She also speaks at school and *tzedakah* gatherings. There are workshops for mothers about parenting, natural health and dealing with stress; for teens there are workshops on building confidence. If you are interested in more information or if you would like to share your stories with the world by having them appear in the next book, send a self-addressed envelope to: Roiza Weinreich, 625 Avenue L, Brooklyn, N.Y. 11230.

NOTES

NOTES

NOTES

NOTES

NOTES

NOTES